The Taste of
IRELAND
Landscape, Culture & food

Publisher and Creative Director: Nick Wells
Project Editor: Victoria Lyle
Picture Research: Victoria Lyle
Art Director: Mike Spender
Digital Design and Production: Chris Herbert
Layout Design: Dave Jones

Special thanks to: Cat Emslie, Anna Groves, Rebecca Kidd, Amanda Leigh, Sara Robson, Sam Shore

13 12

3 5 7 9 10 8 6 4

This edition first published 2009 by
FLAME TREE PUBLISHING
Crabtree Hall, Crabtree Lane
Fulham, London SW6 6TY

www.flametreepublishing.com

Pictures courtesy of: **Corbis** and: Tom Bean 154; Charles Bowman/Robert Harding World Imagery 24–25; Joe Cornish/Arcaid 128; Aidan Crawley/epa 85;
Richard Cummins 141; Jacqui Hurst 135; The Irish Image Collection 92, 122, 124–125, 162; Michael Jenner/Robert Harding World Imagery 123; Justin Kernoghan/epa
40; Barry Lewis 175; Duncan Maxwell/Robert Harding World Imagery 18; Denis O'Regan 89; Hugh Rooney/Eye Ubiquitous 34; Geray Sweeney 17; Tim Thompson 44;
Stefano Torrione/Hemis 60; Kirsty Umback 88; Sandro Vannini 167; Adam Woolfitt 176; **Food Features**: 189; **Foundry Arts**: 46, 48, 49, 146, 148, 184, 185, 186, 187, 188;
The Irish Image Collection: 14, 15, 16, 20–21, 23, 30, 32, 33, 35, 38, 39, 42–43, 45, 67, 68–69, 71, 72–73, 78, 79, 80, 81, 82–83, 84, 87, 90, 91, 93, 94–95, 96, 97, 98, 99,
100, 101, 114, 116–17, 120–21, 127, 132, 133, 134, 136, 137, 138, 139, 140, 155, 156, 157, 158, 160–61, 163, 164–65, 166, 169, 172, 173, 174, 177, 178, 179; **iStock** and:
Alasdair James 19; maciah07 27; Robert Mayne 26, 28, 29; nikon401 61; Alan Tobey 119; **Practical Pictures**: 50, 51, 52, 53, 102, 103, 104, 105, 106, 107, 108, 109, 142,
143, 144, 145, 180, 181, 182, 183; **Shutterstock** and: Nigel Carse 31; L. Kelly 22, 66, 70, 115; Thierry Maffeis 62; Jane McIlroy 64, 129; Monkey Business Images 47, 147,
149; nhtg 65; Panaspics 58, 74; Darren Pierse Kelly 63; Matt Ragen 159; Marco Regalia 126; Andrea Seemann 59; Trutta55 75; walshphotos 118, 168;
TopFoto and: EMPICS 86; UPP 41

Printed in China

Tamsin Pickeral (author) spent her childhood summers in Ireland with her grandparents.
She went on to study art and history of art, and lived for some time in Italy furthering her appreciation
of the subject. She now specializes in books on art and horsemanship with recent publications including
The Horse; 30,000 Years of the Horse in Art, *The Horse Owner's Bible* and *1001 Paintings*.
She is also the author of Flame Tree Publishing's *The Secrets of Britain* and *Best-Kept Secrets of Tuscany*.

The Taste of
IRELAND
Landscape, Culture & food

Tamsin Pickeral

FLAME TREE
PUBLISHING

Contents

Munster

Connacht

Introduction

IRELAND is a country whose breathtaking beauty and landscape is matched by the richness of her heritage and traditional culture. She is divided into four provinces, Ulster, Leinster, Munster and Connacht, each of which is characterized by their landscape and cultural traditions. The geography of each province is further divided into a number of counties. To the north of Ireland there occurs a natural division called the Drumlin Belt, a glacial terrain of hills, rivers and lakes, that roughly marks the boundary between Northern Ireland and the southern Republic of Ireland, or Eire. Northern Ireland comprises six Ulster counties, and the remaining three together with the provinces of Leinster, Munster and Connacht make up southern Ireland.

She is an island defined by diversity and extremes, from her majestic mountains, such as the Macgillycuddy's Reeks range of County Kerry in the far south, to the rich and fertile swathes of land across County Meath in the east, which support the area's thriving horse-breeding industry. The Curragh, a 5,000-acre tract of sandy grasslands in County Kildare to the south of Meath, is famous as the Irish home of horse-racing and the site of evidence of Ireland's ancient past, but these light and fertile soils are the polar opposite of the vast areas of deep, dark bog land in the west. These wet and heavy areas, which are important wildlife havens and are still used for extracting peat, hold their own keys to Ireland's past, buried deep beneath the surface. Nowhere has this become more apparent than in Ceide Fields, on the north Mayo coast in western Ireland, where

excavations of the bog lands have uncovered the oldest-known field system of agriculture in the world, which dates to around 5,000 years ago, and pre-dates both the Egyptian pyramids and Stonehenge in England.

The extraordinary limestone landscape of the Burren in County Clare to the west of Ireland, with its giant rock paving slabs, vertiginous cliffs and labyrinthine caves, is dramatically different from the valleys of coastal County Derry in Northern Ireland. The scenery changes again as the valleys lead from the Sperrin Mountains to the shores of the great Lough Neagh, Ireland's largest lake, and on to her Atlantic coastline of dunes and sweeping sandy beaches. The coastal area of County Antrim in the northern tip of Ireland is home to the spectacular Giant's Causeway and is where crumbling ruins like the Viking stronghold Dunluce Castle bravely cling on to clifftops. And coastal Cork in southern Ireland offers something different again, with her beautiful and rugged coves, small, brightly painted fishing villages and one of the largest natural harbours in the world.

This extraordinary and moving landscape of such disparate parts is united by one natural feature, which has to a great extent shaped her perimeter and interior, namely water. Ireland is covered by a network of rivers, some large and imposing like the River Shannon, the country's largest river, which effectively divides the west of Ireland from the east, and the River Liffey, which flows through the middle of Dublin, capital of the Republic of Ireland. Smaller rivers criss-cross the interior of the country, feeding her many lakes, or loughs. Some of these are vast, shimmering expanses, so big that they house their own collection of islands. Lough Neagh in the centre of Northern Ireland is 392 sq km (151 sq miles) and the largest in the British Isles, while Lough Corrib in County Galway in the Republic of Ireland is the second largest lake in all of Ireland and is connected to the sea at Galway City by the River Corrib. Apart from Ireland's rivers, which have gouged their mark on the landscape, her coastline too has been continuously eroded by the surrounding waters. The unforgiving Atlantic has battered it into one of many nooks and crannies, coves and cliffs, as well as expansive beaches. The west coast boasts a particularly stunning landscape, typified by its many peninsulas such as the Dingle Peninsula (County Kerry), home to numerous pre-historic sites, the Beára Peninsula (Counties Kerry and Cork) and the Iveragh Peninsula (County Kerry), home to Ireland's highest mountain peak, Carrauntoohil. Dotted around her coastline are many islands, some tiny and uninhabited apart from teeming birdlife, while others, such as the Aran Islands in the mouth of Galway Bay off the west coast, are populated and boast their own history and culture entwined with that of mainland Ireland. Water too in the form of rain has had and continues to have a profound effect on the country, promoting the lush nature of her vegetation. It is no small surprise that Ireland is often referred to as the 'Emerald Isle'.

Ireland's social history is long, vibrant, colourful and bloody, dating back to around 7,000 BC when the first settlers are thought to have put down roots. Excavations at Mount Sandel in County Derry, Northern Ireland in 1973–77 uncovered evidence of four large huts with artefacts that carbon dating put to approximately 7,000 BC. Ireland's countryside is littered with evidence of pre-historic civilizations, many of which date to between approximately 4,000–2,000 BC including the World Heritage Site of *Brú na Bóinne* in County Meath, southern Ireland, and the stone-age cemetery at Carrowmore, County Sligo. Much of early Irish history is bound up with legend and folklore, such as the tale of the Giant Finn McCool and his causeway on the north-east coastline, and the warring Fir Bolg peoples who arrived around 4,000 BC and feature in much Irish mythology. They are believed to have crossed into Ireland from Scotland, having first fled oppression and slavery at the hands of the Greeks. Their greatest King was Eochaid, who reputedly

made all rain fall as dew and dictated that every year would yield harvest. Even the country's name derives from a Goddess, the Goddess Ériu, whose modern form is pronounced *Eire*, with the Anglo-Saxon word *land* added.

Christianity arrived in Ireland relatively slowly and in the form of St Palladius during the fifth century. His missonary work has been overshadowed by the fame of St Patrick, who also appeared in the fifth century and was later made the patron saint of Ireland. Monasteries were built across the country, many in remote and isolated spots such as the seventh-century monastery that clings to the cliff-face of Skellig Michael, a rocky island off the south-west coast of Ireland. Although Christianity was dominating pagan worship by the sixth and seventh centuries, there appears to have been an attitude of some tolerance. Pagan ritual sites, most significantly at the mountain now called Croagh Patrick, were not destroyed by Christian crusaders, but were instead adopted into their own culture. Croagh Patrick is now associated with St Patrick who fasted there for 40 days and is a place of Christian pilgrimage. Despite Ireland's continuing strong

Christian affiliations, there remains evidence of Celtic Druid culture and pagan worship, aspects of which are discernible in some of the Irish festivals, such as County Kerry's magical Puck Fair, which takes place every August.

Part of Ireland's mesmerizing charm is her balance of inspired story-telling with cold, hard facts. There is a strong tradition of folk tales and mythology that weaves an inescapable sense of magic around many of her sites and landscape. Irish culture too has remained undeniably prevalent throughout the country. Certain areas are referred to as the Gaeltacht, and here Irish is spoken as the primary language and traditions are clung to fast. The Gaeltacht runs primarily up the western coast of the Republic of Ireland and is defined by its sense of Irishness undiminished by modern influence.

Central to the continuation of Irish culture is an awareness possessed by its people of their heritage and its importance. One of the primary ways in which traditional culture is kept alive is through the year-round festivals and fairs held the length and breadth of the country. Some of these festivities, such as St Patrick's Day in March, are religious in essence, while others have their roots in ancient pagan traditions such as the celebration of May Day, or County Kerry's Puck Fair. They nearly all feature traditional Irish music, dancing, pageantry, drinking and feasting. Irish music and dance are entwined through the course of history, both performances forming an important part of pre-historic pagan rituals and ceremonies. Both have enjoyed a recent resurgence in popularity, particularly in the United States of America, partly due to the success of the theatre productions *River Dance* and *Lord of the Dance*.

Aspects of rural life and agriculture, which have formed such an important part of Ireland's history and economy, are also celebrated through many shows and fairs, one of the most famous of which is the Ballinasloe Horse Fair that takes place in County Galway. A fairly consistent theme of many of the festivals and fairs is that of imbibing two of Ireland's most famous exports, Guinness and Irish Whiskey, and she plays host to a generous quotient of pubs per capita. Many nations, not least the United States, have attempted to duplicate the Irish Pub, but never with quite the same success as the original ones, which remain quintessentially unspoilt and Irish to the core.

Ulster

BUSHMILLS WHISKEY
us over ...ears.

Landscapes

IRELAND is a country of magnificent contrasts, seen nowhere more obviously than in the province of Ulster. Ulster comprises six counties in Northern Ireland and three counties in the Republic of Ireland. Within an area of almost 25,000 sq km (15,534 sq miles), the scenery ranges from craggy, wild coastlines, such as that near Portrush in County Antrim, to the lush, fertile, rolling folds of land seen across parts of Derry and Donegal. Here lies the largest lake in Ireland, Lough Neagh, and the Sperrin Mountain range, an area of dramatic beauty with plunging valleys, crashing rivers and dark, stately forests.

This landscape of unequalled tranquility has been the scene of past devastating violence. Ulster's interior bears the scars from centuries of warring, most notoriously between the Catholics and the Protestant English, brought to the fore in 1601 at the Battle of Kinsale, when the British took Ulster and the rest of Ireland under Elizabeth I of England (1533–1603). Four hundred years earlier, Ulster's shores had been invaded by the Normans, and previous to this, the fearsome Gaelic clans and dynasties fought their own battles in the inevitable struggle for power, wealth and land.

Ulster's magical landscape frequently reflects the imprint of her past, enshrined in history and folklore. This is seen to wonderful effect in the Giant's Causeway, a staircase of monolithic, basalt columns that rise from the shores of County Antrim, which is said to have been built by Fingal the giant. Equally, her sweeping and magnificent countryside is dotted with ancient, often-crumbling castles like the mediaeval Dunluce Castle, or mystical remnants of earlier civilisations as seen in the Bronze Age Beaghmore Stone Circles.

County Fermanagh

The magical County Fermanagh is often and quite justly referred to as Ireland's Lake District. Situated in the most western corner of Northern Ireland, the county is home to the beautiful River Erne that wends its way through the middle of the area and opens into Lake Erne, which is possibly the most famous attraction of Fermanagh. Surrounding the lake are swathes of breathtaking countryside, dotted with natural and historical monuments. Drawn by the crystal waters and the shelter of surrounding forests, the lake is thought to have attracted pre-Christian settlers. Lake Erne is in its essence the 'heart' of the county, while to the west unfolds a series of spectacular limestone hills, which are home to a network of natural tunnels and caves that hold their own enticing secrets.

The county is permeated with a sense of history and magic, much of which centres around Lake Erne and her many islands. Boa Island can be found near the north shore of lower Lake Erne, and is home to two extraordinary sculpted figures: one a double-headed effigy (possibly female), and one a single-headed and probably female figure, which was moved to Boa Island from the nearby Lustymore Island in 1939. Both figures are believed to be pagan Celtic deities, although their date is uncertain, somewhere between the pre-Christian period to the seventh century AD. In contrast, situated off the east coast of lower Lake Erne, is White Island, which is also home to eight carved figures, known to be of Christian origin. There are the surviving remains of an ancient church on the island, including a Romanesque doorway arch and indications of an even earlier monastic settlement.

Janus Stone, Boa Island, Lake Erne

North-West Ulster

Ireland has an endlessly fascinating and ancient past, strikingly evident in the north-west of Ulster. This area boasts two sites of extraordinary historic interest, as well as an untamed and hauntingly beautiful landscape. Lying around the foothills of the Sperrin Mountains and dotted across the counties of Fermanagh, Tyrone and Derry is a number of intricate Bronze Age stone circles thought to date to around 1600 BC. The most famous of these is in Tyrone at Beaghmore, discovered in the early 1940s when the area was used for peat cutting. The stones, of which 1,269 were found, were not fully excavated until 1965, and it remains entirely possibly that the dark peaty soils hold still more. The seven circles, of which six are in pairs, are composed of small stones and are notably irregular. Their function is uncertain, but is thought to relate to social or religious gatherings, or possibly to indicate a burial site.

There is no question over the function of north-west Ulster's other extraordinary monument. The Grianan Aileach rises with majestic splendour at the mouth of the Inishowen Peninsula in County Donegal, its massive stonewalls defiantly punctuating the skyline. The fortress was built on the site of an earlier structure dedicated to pagan worship dated to somewhere between 1700 and 5 BC. However, in the fifth century AD the extant fortress was constructed by the O'Neill dynasty, who were the kings of Aileach, and who shared kingship of Ireland with the southern faction of the O'Neill family. In 1101 the fortress was sacked in a revenge attack by Muircheartach O'Brien, king of Munster, and lay in ruins until it was partially restored in 1870.

Grianan Aileach, County Donegal

Counties Donegal & Derry

Donegal and Derry sit in the north-western and northern-most parts of Ulster, with Donegal being one of Ulster's counties that falls within the Republic of Ireland. Despite their respective allegiances, there are close ties, not only geographically, but also culturally and economically. Donegal occupies an unusual position, being the northern-most county in Ireland and surrounded by the counties of Northern Ireland, with the exception of only one border, which it shares with southern Ireland, or the Republic of Ireland. This apparent isolation has led Donegal to develop a character very much its own. It is one of the most mountainous and untamed counties of Ulster, with the Derryveagh and Bluestack mountains rambling across the countryside in the north and south respectively.

Both Donegal and Derry are counties of spectacular beauty and landscape, often of a wild nature, and notable for their fertile farmland. Derry is also a county of mountains and valleys, with the unruly Sperrin Mountains sprawling across the southern part of the county and opening out onto the lush valleys of the Bann and Foyle rivers, while to the north the landscape is one of sheer cliffs and panoramic beaches. It is to one of these cliffs, near Castlerock, that the brave Mussenden Temple clings. It was built in 1785 by Frederick Augustus Hervey, the 4th Earl of Bristol and Bishop of Derry (1730–1803) to house his library, and was modelled on the Temple of Vesta, Rome, Italy. Erosion of the cliff-face has brought the building perilously close to the edge, where it now perches precariously, although efforts by the National Trust ensure its continued safety.

Farmers riding a tractor, County Donegal

Next page: Gortahork, County Donegal

Coastal Antrim

At the north-east tip of Ulster, overlooking the surging waters of the North Channel, lies the coastal area of Antrim. Her shores are outstandingly beautiful, matched by the Antrim Glens, a range of mountains and valleys that tumble from the Antrim plateau down to the rugged coastline. The nine glens, or valleys, are a popular destination for walkers, drawn by their sublime magnificence and quiet, brooding forests. Areas such as Layde, with her ruined thirteenth-century church and secluded coastal location, Fairhead, Northern Ireland's sheerest cliff-face at around 183 m (600 ft), and the haunting ruins of Dunluce Castle, once a Viking stronghold before being rebuilt by the Normans, only to partially tumble into the sea in 1629, are just some of the delights that coastal Antrim has to offer.

There is, however, one natural feature of Antrim's coastline against which the others could be said to pale. The Giant's Causeway is a sight so breathtaking and extraordinary that it is rated as the fourth natural wonder in the United Kingdom. Around 38,000 hexagonal, basalt columns rise majestically from the coastline, some 12 m (39 ft) or so from the ground and form what appears to be a great stairway. In real terms they are the result of lava flows cooling and solidifying some 60 million years ago, although the various legends provide a more stimulating

Atlantic Coastline near Portrush. Next Page: Giant's Causeway

explanation. According to one legend, the causeway was built by the Giant Fingal who wished to create a pathway across the sea to his beloved who lived on the Scottish island of Staffa. Another tale recalls that the Giant Finn (Finn McCool) built the path to reach his Scottish rival Benandonner.

Central Belfast

The city of Belfast lies to the east of Ulster and at the mouth of the river Lagan, which flows into the Bay of Belfast. Its name comes from the Irish 'Bealfeirste', meaning 'crossing at the estuary'. The city is the capital of Northern Ireland and, despite its turbulent history, particularly through 'The Troubles' (c. 1969–late 1990s), it remains defiantly optimistic, buoyed most recently by a period of sustained calm.

History reverberates through the city's wide streets, whose foundations were built on the site of a Bronze Age settlement. Surrounding Belfast is evidence of pre-historic inhabitation, from the 5,000-year-old Giant's Ring near Shaw's Bridge, to the Iron Age hill forts scattered across the adjacent countryside. However, it was not until around 1657 that the city really began to flourish, with industries in linen and ship-building being started by Scottish Presbyterian immigrants. Through the eighteenth and nineteenth centuries Belfast grew as a commercial and industrial centre, and in the early twentieth century was responsible for one of the world's most famous ships, the *Titanic*, which was built there between 1909–12.

The city, which has a quiet and understated grandeur, is home to many notable buildings and monuments including the City Hall, finished in 1906, and the recent addition of the Belfast Eye

Albert Memorial Clock Tower

adjacent to the hall, built in 2007 and due to be dismantled in 2009. One of the most lavish buildings in the city is the former Ulster Bank in Waring St, built in 1860, although the Crown Liquor Saloon, designed in 1876, is also exquisitely ornate and is one of the finest high-Victorian saloons in the United Kingdom.

Belfast Environs

The growth of Belfast, rapid in the nineteenth century, is now to some extent limited by its geography. The city sits at the mouth of the River Lagan at the western end of Lough Belfast and is surrounded to the north and north-west by mountains, including Black Mountain, Divis Mountain and Cavehill, the last of which is reputed to have been the inspiration for Jonathan Swift's (1667–1745) *Gulliver's Travels*. These natural boundaries effectively mark the extent of the city's spread. Belfast is divided into areas, with the city centre forming the heart and others radiating outwards. These have been designated as different cultural areas in a large part to boost tourism.

The stunning Botanic Gardens can be found in the Queen's Quarter in southern Belfast. They were opened in 1828 and provide residents and visitors with 28 acres of beautifully manicured parkland and glasshouses, of which the Palm House, finished in 1840, is of particular note. To the east of Belfast, the magnificent Northern Ireland Parliament buildings, known as Stormont, can be found. The original plans for the building were even more lavish and were reminiscent of the designs for the Capitol building in Washington DC, USA. However, following the catastrophic stock market crash in 1929, the plans were reworked, omitting the dome and greatly simplified, with Stormont eventually being finished in 1932. It is of some interest that in 2005 the Great Hall of the building was used for the funeral of the footballer George Best (1946–2005). This marked the first time since the end of the First World War that the building was used for any non-political or non-governmental function.

Stormont

Palm House, Belfast Botanic Gardens

Ards Peninsula

The long and narrow stretch of land that is the Ards Peninsula can be found on the north-eastern coast of Ulster, and is bordered on one side by the large Strangford Lough, and on the other by the turbulent North Channel. For such a relatively small piece of land, the peninsula is home to many wonderful sites, both manmade and natural, and is also a wildlife haven.

At the northern-most end of the peninsula and Lough Strangford, and sitting just inland from it, is the town of Newtownards, the largest town of the Ards region. Documented history of the town dates to AD 545 and the establishment of a monastery, although it is believed the area had been settled previously to this. It is a place full of history and beauty, seen particularly in the nearby Mount Stewart, an eighteenth-century house that was home to the Vane-Tempest-Stewart family. The house is impressive enough, but even more striking are the landscaped grounds, which include several separate gardens and the 'Dodo Terrace', featuring a collection of wonderful and imaginative stone animals.

To the west of Newtownards the skyline is dominated by Scrabo Tower, a folly built in 1857 as a memorial to the Third Marquis of Londonderry. On the east shore of the Lough is Grey Abbey with its Cistercian Abbey, founded in 1193 by Affreca, wife of the Christian Knight John de Courcy (1160–1219), which now sadly lies in ruins. The remains of another abbey can be seen at Inch Abbey on the north bank of the river Quoile, and to the south of Lough Strangford.

Scrabo Tower, County Down

County Down

County Down is one of Ulster's jewels. It was described by Percy French in his famous song as where 'the Mountains of Mourne sweep down to the sea'. The town of Newcastle nestles at the foot of the Mourne Mountains, sandwiched between their lofty heights and a five-mile stretch of shoreline. Most impressive is Slieve Donard, the highest mountain in Northern Ireland at 849 m (2,785 ft), which was named after St Donard, a follower of St Patrick.

St Patrick (*c.* AD 387–461) is closely identified with County Down, and is said to be buried at Down Cathedral in Downpatrick, which sits at the southern end of Lough Strangford. Legend relates him sailing into the neighbouring town of Saul in AD 432, where he converted the locals to Christianity.

To the south-east of Downpatrick is the small, but flourishing village of Ardglass, famous for its prawns and herrings, and still an important centre of fishing. It is also home to Jordan's Castle, a fifteenth-century tower house, and to the fifteenth-century Ardtole Church, which looks across the Irish Sea and the Isle of Man.

Another town of note is Banbridge, which sits along the Upper Bann River, with its wide streets and pleasant aspect. In 1834

an underpass, thought to be the first structure of its kind, was designed and implemented by William Dargan (1799–1867) to run beneath the steep main street allowing the stagecoach horses an easier passage. Between Banbridge and the market town of Rathfriland is an area known as Brontë Homeland, named after Patrick Brontë (1777–1861), father of Anne (1820–49), Charlotte (1816–55) and Emily (1818–48), who were born in the area.

Kilkeel Harbour

Mourne Mountains

County Armagh

County Armagh is the smallest of Ulster's counties and is widely regarded as the spiritual home of Ireland, for it is here in the town of Armagh that the Roman Catholic and Church of Ireland leaders are based. The Church of Ireland cathedral, dedicated to St Patrick, rests on the top of a small hill where the saint is reputed to have founded his first church in AD 443. Opposite, on the summit of another hill, sits the Catholic cathedral, also dedicated to St Patrick, striking with its pale neo-Gothic exterior. Before the rise of Christianity, the town was a centre of Celtic pagan worship, which is traced to the nearby Navan Fort (or *Emain Macha*), seen today as a circular enclosure. Within this is a smooth knoll of earth beneath which is hidden an inner structure of timber and limestone blocks, and an impression of a ring barrow. The name is taken from the mythological goddess Macha.

The landscape of the county is one of contrasts: the steep Slieve Gullion, an extinct volcano in the south, and the Carrigatuke, Lislea and Camlough mountains; the undulating Drumlin hills of the centre; and the flat plains in the north that lead down to the shores of Lough Neagh. The lough is the largest lake in the British Isles and is particularly noted for the number and variety of its birds.

County Armagh is one of the most fertile areas of Ulster and has earned the name 'Orchard County' on account of its thriving apple-growing industry. Apple orchards stretch as far as the eye can see across the plains of Armagh, and in the spring time are awash with blossom.

Apple orchard

Culture

ULSTER is quite unique within Ireland because it is the only province to contain both Northern Irish (six) and Republic of Ireland (three) counties. Furthermore, the whole of Northern Ireland is made by six of Ulster's counties, so despite the very definitive political demarcation between 'North' and 'South', there is very little obvious difference in cultural aspects within the province.

One of the most predominant influences on Ulster's culture is that of the Scottish. The Scottish Mull of Kintyre is only a short 19 kms (12 miles) away from the coast of Country Antrim, both being within clear view of each other, and this geographic proximity has contributed greatly to the exchange of people, culture and ideas through history. The links between Scottish and Irish dance, language, sports, traditions, crafts and even whiskey (in Scottish, whisky) are clearly discernible, while both cultures share a similarly stoical and practical outlook on life.

For centuries before the Plantation Act of 1609 under James I of England, Scotland and Ireland (1566–1625), the Scottish and Irish of the Ulster region traded lands and customs. During this attempt to 'civilize' Ulster, many estates were confiscated from the Irish and given to the English and lowland Scottish. While for many English the Ulster climate and agriculture was unforgiving, for the lowland farmers from Scotland the lands were a great improvement on those they had tilled back home. The relationship of the Ulster Irish and the Scottish grew and strengthened over the centuries, while a cross-cultural exchange took place culminating in the very close ties between the two cultures today.

Irish Whiskey

There are few things quite so synonymous with Irish culture as Irish whiskey, which is surely the best of its kind in the world. The history of whiskey in Ireland is one that dates back to antiquity and is perhaps surprisingly linked to the church. The first distilleries are believed to have been founded by monks, although the first licensed distillery was not opened until 1608. This was Bushmills, the oldest whiskey distillery in the world, which is still active today.

By the eighteenth and nineteenth centuries, the drink had become extremely popular in Britain, and the Irish whiskey industry, much of it unlicensed and illegal, was flourishing. By 1900, Irish whiskey was the top spirit exported to Britain, and was also being exported to the West Indies and the United States of America. However, the combined developments in Scottish whisky and the drop in the US market due to prohibition brought the Irish whiskey industry to its knees, and by the 1960s the export of whiskey had dwindled to virtually nothing. Three surviving distilleries joined forces to create Irish Distillers (IDL), but some years later IDL and the Bushmills Distillery were bought out by Seagrams, who then sold them to the French company Pernod Richard. Bushmills was later bought by Diageo and today the Cooley Distillery, established in 1989, is the only all-Irish owned distillery.

Old Bushmills advertising

The word 'whiskey' comes from the Gaelic term '*uisce beatha*', which rather aptly translates as 'water of life'. The 'e' of the Irish spelling was adopted in the 1840s to distinguish the allegedly superior-quality whiskey from its poorer Scotch relative.

Competitors in the 2000 World Irish Dancing Championships at the Belfast Waterfront hall, County Antrim

Irish Dance

Irish dance has enjoyed a recent surge in popularity due in great part to the fantastic productions of *River Dance* and *Lord of the Dance*, and the magical footwork of Jean Butler (b. 1971) and Michael Flatley (b. 1958). The history of Irish dance stretches back to pre-Christian times, and it is believed that early Irish dances evolved alongside the development of Irish music, in conjunction with pagan rituals and ceremonies. Dance was subject to a wide variety of influences brought to Ireland by immigrants from the continent, especially the Celts, and later the Normans during the conquests of the twelfth century, as seen in the *quadrille*, a dance performed by four couples in a square formation.

Irish dancing grew to embrace several distinct forms, which by the sixteenth century included the Irish Hey, the Rinnce Fada (long dance) and the Trenchmore. Dances were performed during important ceremonies, annual festivals, fetes, weddings and even at funerals. During the eighteenth century Irish Dance Masters began to appear. These travelling performers would visit different villages and towns, teaching the complicated dance steps to the local inhabitants. Dance Masters were greatly revered, and set about formalizing aspects of the different dances, introducing rules and choreographing different steps. It was also during the eighteenth century that

Michael Flatley with the cast of his show *Lord of the Dance*.   Next page: Irish dancing, County Derry

solo dances appeared. In 1929 the Irish Dance Commission was formed and regulated the different types of Irish dance such as the jig, reel, hornpipe, set and step, laying down rules for competitions. Dance competitions or *feis*, in which competitors still wear traditional costume and shoes, are extremely popular today in Ireland and the USA, with national and world championship events.

Ulster Craft

The tradition of rural crafts in Ulster remains strong, with two crafts in particular being associated with the area. These are linen making and weaving, and pottery. Historically, linen is one of the oldest cloths to be woven, with remarkably intact swatches discovered in ancient Egyptian tombs. The history of linen in Ulster is not quite as long, but for the last three to four hundred years the area has been famed for its linen production. Ulster is one of the main linen producers in Western Europe, and 'Irish linen' is one of the highest-quality and most sought-after. Linen, which comes from the flax plant, began as a cottage industry. By the eighteenth century, linen production was becoming slightly more industrial and, in 1711, the Board of Trustees of the Linen Manufacturers of Ireland was established. It was through this that the high standards recognised today were laid down.

The production of pottery is the other major Ulster tradition, with the Belleek Pottery, County Fermanagh being the most famous centre for the craft. The pottery was established in 1857 and originally made only fine ware pottery, which is pottery made from tin-glazed earthenware or porcelain. Later they concentrated solely on the production of porcelain. This type of pottery requires fine, white clay, which naturally occurs in parts of Ireland. Shortly after opening, the Belleek Pottery won the contract to supply the insulators for the telegraph poles being erected all over the country, which saw the company flourish. The Belleek Pottery is still very much a leader in its industry today, but Ulster is also home to many fine smaller potteries producing exquisite hand-crafted pieces.

Ceramicist working on Parian ware vases, Belleek Pottery, County Fermanagh

Weaving, County Donegal

Champ

INGREDIENTS

910 g/2 ¼ lb/5 cups potatoes, peeled and halved

235 ml/8 fl oz/1 cup milk

1 bunch spring onions/scallions, thinly sliced

½ tsp of salt, or to taste

55 g/2 oz/¼ cup butter

freshly ground black pepper, to taste

1 Place the potatoes into a large pot, and fill with enough water to cover. Bring to a boil, and cook until tender, about 20 minutes.

2 Drain well. Return to very low heat and allow the potatoes to dry out for a few minutes. It helps if you place a clean dishtowel over the potatoes to absorb any remaining moisture.

3 Meanwhile, heat the milk and spring onions/scallions gently in a saucepan, until warm.

4 Mash the potatoes, salt and butter together until smooth. Stir in the milk and spring onions until evenly mixed. Season with freshly ground black pepper. Make a well in the centre of the potato and place in this a knob of butter. Garnish with a few extra spring onions/scallions, then serve.

ORIGINS AND TRADITIONS

Champ, also known as poundies, cally or pandy, is an Irish favourite that originates in Ulster, although there are many regional variations.

Irish Apple Cake

CUTS INTO 8-10 SLICES

INGREDIENTS

225 g/8 oz/2 cups self-raising flour

1½ tsp baking powder

150 g/5 oz/½ cup margarine, softened

150 g/5 oz/¾ cup caster/superfine sugar, plus extra for sprinkling

1 tsp vanilla essence/extract

2 large eggs, beaten

1.1 kg/2½ lb/7 cups tart cooking apples such as Bramley or Grenadier, peeled, cored and sliced

1 tbsp lemon juice

½ tsp ground cinnamon

fresh custard sauce or cream, to serve

ORIGINS AND TRADITIONS

County Armagh, in Ulster, is known as the 'Orchard County'. Numerous apple festivals are held in the county throughout the year and many popular apple recipes originate from Armagh.

1 Preheat the oven to 170°C/325°F/Gas Mark 3 10 minutes before baking. Lightly oil and line the base of a 20.5 cm/8 in deep cake tin/pan with non-stick baking parchment. Sift the flour and baking powder into a small bowl.

2 Beat the margarine, sugar and vanilla essence/extract until light and fluffy. Gradually beat in the eggs a little at a time, beating well after each addition. Stir in the flour.

3 Spoon about one-third of the mixture into the tin, smoothing the surface. Toss the apple slices in the lemon juice and cinnamon and spoon over the cake mixture, making a thick, even layer. Spread the remaining mixture over the apple layer to the edge of the tin, making sure the apples are covered. Smooth the top with the back of a wet spoon and sprinkle generously with sugar.

4 Bake in the preheated oven for 1½ hours, or until the cake is well risen and golden, the apples are tender and the centre of the cake springs back when pressed lightly. (Reduce the oven temperature slightly and cover the cake loosely with foil if the top browns too quickly.)

5 Transfer to a wire rack and cool for about 20 minutes in the tin. Run a thin knife blade between the cake and the tin to loosen the cake and invert on to a paper-lined rack. Turn the cake the right way up and cool. Serve with the custard sauce or cream.

Boxty Potato Pancakes

MAKES 4 PANCAKES

INGREDIENTS

450g/1lb/2½ cups potatoes, peeled and chopped

50–75g/2–3oz/½–⅔ cup plain/all-purpose flour

about 150ml/¼ pint/⅔ cup milk

salt to taste

knob of butter

1 Place the peeled and chopped potatoes in a blender or in the bowl of a food processor and process until the potato is thoroughly blended.

2 Add the flour and enough milk to the processed potato to give a dropping consistency and add salt to taste. The milk and flour can be adjusted, depending on how thin you like your pancake. Heat a little butter on a griddle or cast-iron frying pan.

3 Pour about a quarter of the mixture into the pan – if the consistency is right it will spread evenly over the base. Cook over a medium heat for about 5 minutes on each side, depending on the thickness of the cake. Serve rolled with the hot filling of your choice.

ORIGINS AND TRADITIONS

Boxty comes from the northern counties of Ireland and was traditionally eaten on the first day of February, St. Brigid's Day. There is even a popular rhyme about Boxty:

Boxty on the griddle,
Boxty in the pan,
If you can't make boxty,
You'll never get a man.

Yellowman

MAKES ABOUT 900G/2LB

INGREDIENTS

115g/4oz/½ cup butter

2 tbsp vinegar

225g/8oz/scant ⅔ cup treacle/molasses

225g/8oz/scant ⅔ cup golden/light corn syrup

450g/1lb/2 cups demerara/raw sugar

½ tsp bicarbonate of/baking soda, sieved

1 Grease a baking tin/pan. Melt the butter in a pan and add the vinegar, treacle/molasses, syrup and sugar. Stir over a gentle heat until the sugar has completely dissolved, and then raise the heat and bring to a boil.

2 Boil steadily until the mixture reaches soft crack stage – 151°C/304°F on a sugar thermometer.

3 Remove from the heat and stir in the bicarbonate of/baking soda. When it foams up, stir again, then pour into the baking tin/pan and, using a spatula, keep working the edges into the centre until the mixture is pale. Mark up into squares.

ORIGINS AND TRADITIONS

Yellowman is associated with the Ould Lammas Fair of Ballycastle, County Antrim, where it is still sold today.

Leinster

Landscapes

THE BEAUTIFUL and historic province of Leinster stretches down along the eastern seaboard of Ireland, abutting the southern border of Ulster, and on her western sides, the provinces of Connacht and Munster. Leinster is the most densely populated province of Ireland, with the city of Dublin being the jewel in her cosmopolitan crown. But her populous nature does not detract from the inspiring landscape, and human inhabitation has still to mar the enormous reaches of rolling green land, the extent of which are perhaps best appreciated when seen from the air. Unsurprisingly, this area is home to some of Ireland's most ancient settlements; it would seem that our ancestors were naturally drawn to the province, attracted by the cool, clear water supply, the fertile soils and relatively temperate climate.

The pre-history of the region – informed in part by archaeology, in part by legend – recounts its occupation by five warring Fir Bolg tribes, from among whom the Laigin faction rose to dominance, and gave the area its name. Another shadowy historic figure is Hugony the Great, said to have been the first High King of Laigin, who is thought to have ruled in the seventh century BC, and left his mark in the hill fort of *Ailinne Knochawlin*, near Kilcullen, County Kildare.

Leinster is littered with marks of its ancient past: the Hill of Tara in County Westmeath, which served as a ritual centre for kingship and a sacred place since Neolithic times; the Newgrange Passage Tomb, County Meath, a burial mound that dates to around 5,000 years ago; and the legendary Fionn mac Cumhaill's fort at the Hill of Allen, County Kildare.

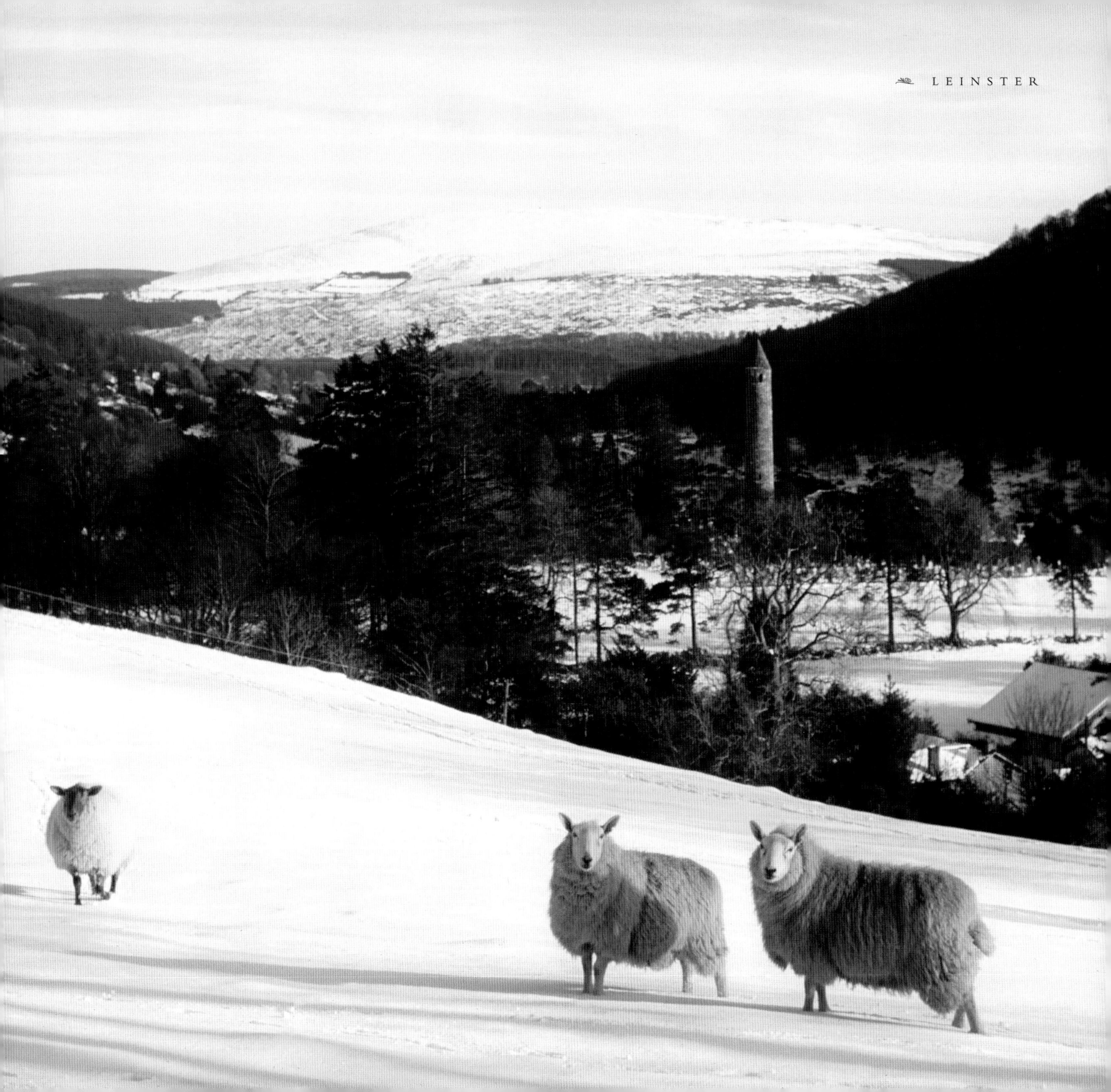

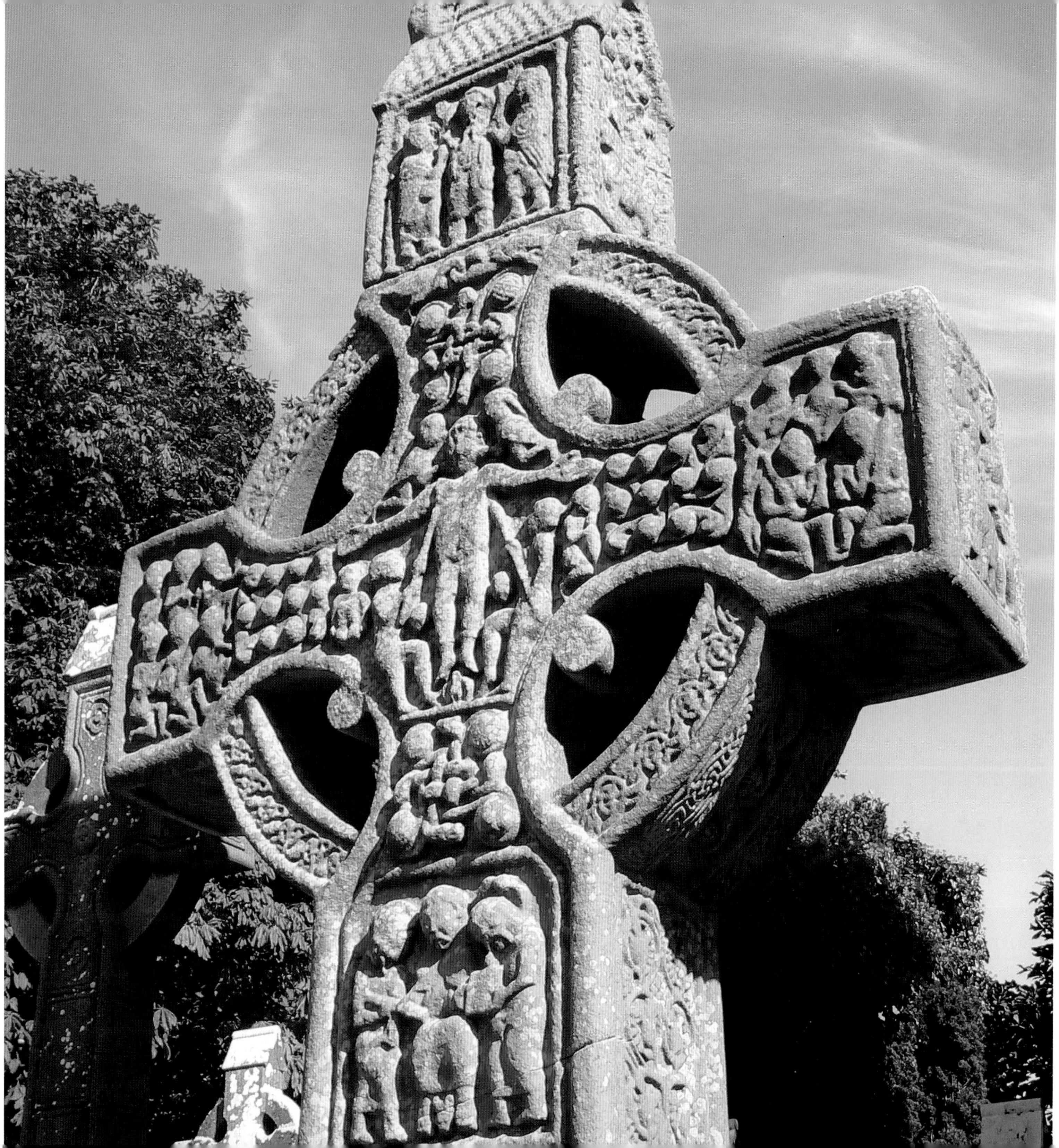

Muireadhach's Cross, Monasterboice, County Louth

North-West Leinster

Tucked away in the north-west of Leinster are two counties that sit just a little way off the tourist trail, despite being home to some of the most fascinating early Christian sites. The 'wee' county of Louth is in the far northern reaches of Leinster and, as its name suggests, is the smallest of the twelve Leinster counties. This small pocket of tranquility became a stronghold of Christian belief. This can still be seen today in the remains of Mellifont Abbey, founded in 1142 and the first Cistercian abbey to be built in Ireland, and the monastery of Monasterboice. Dating back to the late fifth/early sixth century AD, this ancient monastery is home to the Cross of Muireadhach, one of the most impressive stone crosses of its kind and covered in exquisite carvings. The cross dates to between AD 899 and 924, and stands nearly 5.5 m (18 ft) tall.

Clonmacnoise, County Offaly

Equally impressive and idyllic is the north-western county of Offaly. Here the Slieve Bloom mountains in the southern reaches of the region roll down into the impressive flood plains of the River Shannon to the north, while much of the rest of the county is covered in peat bog land. Situated along the mighty Shannon are the remains of the Clonmacnoise monastery, founded in the sixth century by Saint Ciarán. The monastery grew to be a major centre for religious learning, and within the compound eight churches, two round towers, three high crosses and many religious monuments were built. Tragically, Clonmacnoise was overrun by an English garrison from Athlone in 1552, and was left in ruins.

County Meath

The county of Meath originally formed part of the ancient Kingdom of Mide, so called for its central position within Ireland, and was home to several High Kings of Ireland; the county is still sometimes referred to as 'the royal county'. Of particular interest is the Hill of Tara, whose history contains equal measures of fact and legend. This large, pre-historic compound is reputed to have been the seat of the High Kings of Ireland. According to legend, the Kings of Tara were selected through the visions of a druid who slept on the hide of a white bull. Once selected, the candidate drove a chariot pulled by untamed stallions, and if his claim to kingship were true, when the chariot's axle touched a special phallic-shaped stone, the *Lia Fáil*, the stone would let out a scream to be heard through all of Ireland.

Meath is also home to one of the most important megalithic sites in Europe. The site, *Brú na Bóinne*, sits overlooking the River Boyne, and is a complex of barrows, monuments and enclosures, which date to around 5,000 years ago. Of these, the most impressive is the Newgrange Passage tomb. This huge burial mound has a long entrance passage that leads to the centre of the mound, which is cruciform in shape. Three recesses with granite basins sit at the end of the cruciform arms and contain cremated remains, suggesting this is the

Hill of Tara

burial mound of kings or chiefs. Most extraordinary is a 'roof box' above the entrance passageway that allows light to flood the corridor during the sunrise at the winter solstice. The entrance is lit for approximately seventeen minutes, before the sun moves on.

Newgrange Passage Tomb, Brú na Bóinne

Dublin & the River Liffey

Dublin is the largest city in Ireland and also her capital. The area is thought to have been settled around the first century BC, although it was not firmly established until around the ninth century AD. Since then she has developed and evolved into one of the most beautiful and lively cities in Europe. From her beginnings Dublin has been an important centre of commerce, politics and industry. The name derives from the Gaelic '*Dubh linn*', meaning 'black pool', though in the Middle Ages she was also referred to as *Átha Cliath*, 'The Settlement of the Ford of the Reed Hurdles'. This refers to the city's position at the mouth of the majestic River Liffey, which flows from the Wicklow Mountains, across the plains of Kildare and turns eastwards to join the sea at Dublin.

The Liffey divides Dublin into the Northside and the Southside, of which the Northside is considered to be the 'poorer' area. Dublin Castle, much restored, sits in the Southside. The castle was begun in 1208 and largely finished by 1230, with a primarily defensive function. It formed one corner of the old city's perimeter and joined the city's encircling walls, while the River Poddle flowed along two of the castle's sides forming a natural defence. Much of the castle was rebuilt in the eighteenth century. Not far from the castle are Christ Church and St Patrick's, the two Protestant cathedrals originally founded by Norse kings, and next to the castle is the impressive eighteenth-century City Hall, originally the Royal Exchange and designed by Thomas Cooley (1740–84).

Customs House

Central Dublin

Despite the size and bustle of Dublin, her centre remains relatively small. Much of the architectural character and street planning seen today in Dublin was laid out from the seventeenth century onwards and aided by the Wide Streets Commission, which oversaw the development of streets, buildings and bridges. The Georgian period from 1714–1830 saw the emergence of some of Dublin's most beautiful buildings, including the magnificent Customs House, the first major free-standing public building in Dublin with four separate ornate facades, the pedestrian Ha'Penny Bridge, opened in 1816, and the Four Courts building, designed by James Gandon (1743–1823), who also designed the Customs House. It was during this period that many of the city's magnificent squares were also laid out, including Merrion Square, lined with graceful Georgian townhouses and the National Gallery of Art, and once the home of the poet William Butler Yeats (1865–1939). The largest square is St Stephen's Green, built around a beautifully manicured park, complete with statuary and an artificial lake.

Dublin is home to three universities, the most famous of which is the University of Dublin with its Trinity College. The university dates back to 1592, and the beautifully landscaped Trinity College now contains many buildings of both modern and historic architecture, including the Old Library

begun in 1712 and the Dining Room. It is in the Old Library that the famous *Book of Kells*, one of the finest illuminated manuscripts in the world dating to around AD 800, is housed.

Georgian door, Merrion Square

Counties Kildare & Wicklow

Two particularly scenic counties are Kildare, famous for its horse racing, and Wicklow, commonly referred to as the 'Garden of Ireland'. Kildare sits to the south-west of Dublin, right in the heartland of Ireland, and is noted for its fertile soils and lush grass on which the area's thriving horse industry feeds. The county boasts a flourishing tourist industry, much of it based on sporting activities such as horse racing, motor sports and the quieter pursuit of angling, but as with much of Ireland, it is also home to numerous stunning historical buildings and landscaped gardens. One such architectural gem is Athy Castle, situated on the Barrow River and built in 1417 by Sir John Talbot (1384/90–1453). Close by is Woodstock Castle, built in the thirteenth century, but now little more than ruins, and something of a contrast to the splendid Kilkea Castle at Castledermot, which was begun in 1180. Kilkea is now a four-star hotel, and is the oldest continually inhabited castle in Ireland.

Wicklow is south of Dublin and borders Kildare to the west. It is an extraordinarily beautiful county that is traversed by the picturesque Wicklow Mountains, the longest mountain range in Ireland. Crossing the range, though avoiding the major peaks, is the Wicklow Way, which at 132 km (82 miles), is the longest way-marked trail in Ireland.

Glendalough, County Wicklow. Next page: Wicklow Way, County Wicklow

Possibly one of the most striking sites in Wicklow is Glendalough, a stunning glacial valley that holds two crystal-clear lakes. Within the valley are many monuments and remains dating from the Bronze Age to the mediaeval period, including a circular stone fort, several churches and a round tower. The mediaeval monastic settlement was founded by St Kevin in around AD 600, and largely destroyed by English troops in 1398.

Athy Castle, County Kildare

County Wexford

County Wexford nestles in the south-eastern corner of Ireland and is bordered on all sides by natural features. To the south of the county the Atlantic laps its shores, and to the east its beaches tumble into St George's Channel and the Irish Sea. The River Barrow marks the western borders, and to the north are the Blackstairs and Wicklow mountains. The interior of the county is largely low-lying and rural, while along her coastline are dotted fishing villages and towns. The largest town is Wexford, situated at the mouth of the River Slaney. It was first settled in around AD 800 by the Vikings, and remained independent for several hundred years, although this came to an end in 1169 when it was occupied by the Normans.

An area of particular interest in County Wexford is the Hook Peninsula, on the south coast. Here a number of historic sites can be found: the Hook Lighthouse, built in the thirteenth century, and the oldest operational lighthouse in Europe; not far away is the reputedly haunted Loftus Hall, an imposing and faintly eerie structure built in 1870 on the site of the earlier Redmond Hall, built in 1350; then there's Tintern Abbey, an impressive thirteenth-century Cistercian abbey, now in ruins; also Ballyhack Castle, built by the Knights Templar in the fifteenth century; and Duncannon Fort, built in 1588, and now a maritime museum and craft centre.

To the east of the Hook Peninsula and 5 kms (3 miles) offshore are the Saltee Islands, Great Saltee and Little Saltee. Both are uninhabited and privately owned, and form one of Ireland's largest bird sanctuaries.

Hook Lighthouse

Gannets on Saltee Islands. Next page: Wexford City

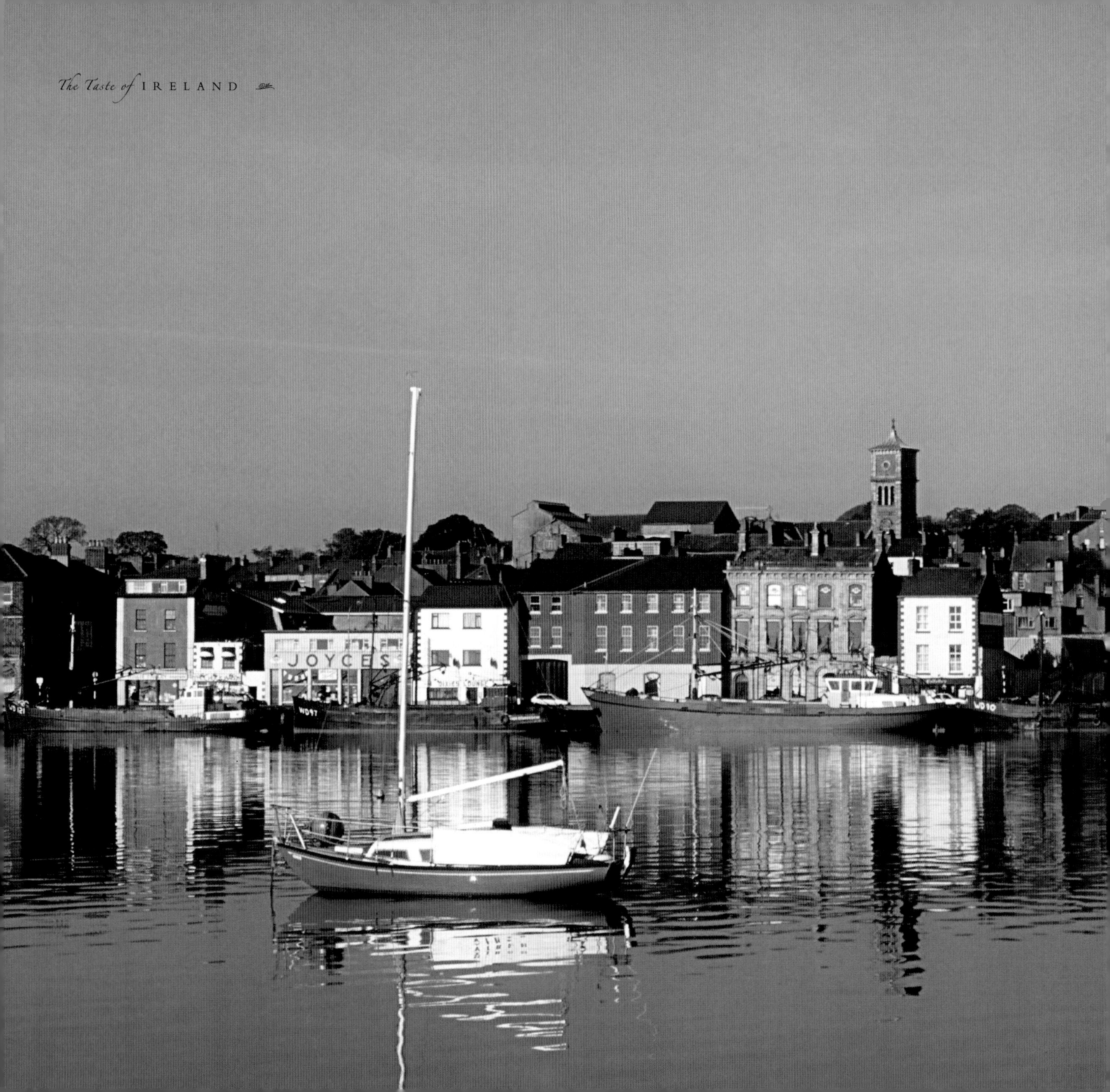
JOYCES
WD121
WD97
WD10

Counties Kilkenny & Carlow

Poppy Field, County Carlow

Both Kilkenny and Carlow, in southern Leinster, share borders with County Wexford. Kilkenny is the larger of the two and is crossed by two major rivers, the Nore and the Suir. It is an area of outstanding beauty and is home to several nature reserves and conservation areas. Dotted across the landscape is a number of distinctive round towers, one of the most impressive of which is at St Canice's Cathedral in the town of Kilkenny, with others interrupting the skyline near Bennettsbridge, Kells and Johnstown.

Kilkenny's most famous castle is Kilkenny Castle, high above the Nore River. The original building was begun in 1192 by William Marshall (1144–1219), and in 1391 it passed into the Butler family until 1967 when, in some state of disrepair, it was presented to the people of Kilkenny and later restored. The town is a lively and historic place that combines mediaeval streets and

buildings with more modern architecture. To the east of the town is Kilkenny College whose famous former pupils include Jonathan Swift (1667–1745) and George Berkeley (1685–1753).

By contrast, County Carlow is one of the smallest counties in Ireland but no less scenic for that. To the east of the county are the dramatic Blackstairs Mountains, while to the west stretch the lush, fertile Barrow Valley and the rolling Killeshin Hills. These hills offer spectacular views across the surrounding countryside and to the county's main town, Carlow. It is a lively and rapidly growing town, home to some fine architectural features. The thirteenth-century ruins of Carlow Castle are worth a visit, as are the town's eighteenth-century courthouse and nineteenth-century cathedral. However, perhaps the county's most impressive manmade feature is the Browne's Hill Dolmen, the largest dolmen in Ireland, dating to around 5,000 years ago.

Culture

IRISH CULTURE is as varied as her landscape, with traditions, festivals and sports current today that can be traced back to pre-history. If anything, the cultural traditions of this small country, and specifically of Leinster, have become more celebrated and practised over time as conscious efforts are made to preserve Irish culture.

Many of these traditions are reflective of their origins. Farming, for example, remains centrally important to Ireland, and it was based on this that early settlers survived. Agricultural fairs play an important part in rural Irish life, and are colourful and lively events that attract many tourists, as well as local communities. Ploughing competitions, both mechanized and horse-driven, take place across Leinster and much of the rest of the country.

Leinster in particular is famous as the home of Irish sport, at the centre of which is horse racing. The province's rich soils and lush grasses sustain a multi-million Euro business, and people travel from far and wide to the Irish races. Aside from racing, Leinster's history is bound to that of Gaelic football and hurling, two ancient Irish sports. Croke Park in Dublin is Ireland's largest sporting stadium, and is Gaelic football's spiritual home and the headquarters of the Gaelic Athletic Association.

Leinster is also host to numerous parades and festivals with ancient precedents, both pagan and Christian, such as the annual May Day festivals based on pagan beliefs and rituals, and the spring celebration of St Patrick's Day, which commemorates the patron saint of Ireland. At these events it is not unusual for quantities of one of Ireland's most famous exports to be drunk. Guinness, the thick, dark stout, which along with whiskey is the lifeblood of Ireland, was developed in Leinster at the Dublin-based St James's Gate Brewery in 1759.

Rural Pursuits

IRELAND remains at its heart a country of agriculture and related rural pursuits. It is part of the country's charm that she has retained such strong ties with her traditional and cultural past, and there are few places in the world that can equal her in this respect.

For many people, two of the strongest associations with Ireland are horses and Guinness, and she excels in the production of both. Her horse industry, much of which is based in Leinster, encompasses the thoroughbred racing industry and the breeding of the ubiquitous Irish Hunter. Hunting, a sport which grew from the need to control pests, is still extremely popular across Ireland. There are over 40 foxhound packs, over 30 harrier packs (whose quarry is hares) and two packs of stag hounds in the country, with County Westmeath in Leinster being a particular hunting stronghold.

Possibly a slightly less famous cultural tradition is that of the ploughing competition. These events take place across Leinster and the rest of the country, and are taken extremely seriously. National and international ploughing competitions are held at different locations each year and attract competitors from all over the world. These competitions are a wonderful opportunity for farmers to showcase their skills and the importance of agriculture. Often they are held alongside other agricultural competitions such as livestock shows and machinery events, or at agricultural fairs, festivals and shows. Although ploughing competitions have been being held in Ireland for hundreds of years, one of the first documented and organised events was in 1931 at Athy, County Kildare. The National Ploughing Association dates to that time.

National Ploughing Championship, County Kildare

The Bray Harriers hunting in County Wicklow

Horse Breeding & Racing

Leinster is the heart and soul of Irish horse breeding and the racing industry. Ireland as a country boasts 27 racecourses, which is more per capita than any other country in the world, an indicator of the importance of this industry within the country. Race days are family affairs, lively, fun and sociable, and form an intrinsic part of Irish culture.

Every racecourse and race meeting in Ireland has its own unique and particular character, such as the famous annual Laytown Races held on the wide sandy beach of Laytown, County Meath. They are the only such races in Europe to be run under official rules, and are said to have been first organized in 1876 by the local parish priest. Race day has to be carefully planned to enable the races to be run while the tide is out, and the area cleared again before the tide comes back in. Possibly the most famous of the area's tracks is the Curragh, whose first recorded race was in 1727. This is the home of 'The Classics', five big races being the Budweiser Irish Derby, the Darley Irish Oaks, the Boylesports 1000 Guineas, the Boylesports 2000 Guineas and the Irish Field St Leger. Not far from the Curragh track is Punchestown, which is one of the most friendly and atmospheric tracks. It is not unusual on race days for the entire town including schools to close to enable everyone to watch. Recently Punchestown has undergone a multi-million Euro re-development, and attracts visitors from all over the world.

Curragh Racecourse, County Kildare

Phoenix Park Racecourse, County Dublin.   Next page: Laytown Races, County Meath

Irish Sport

Ireland vs. Scotland in the Six Nations rugby competition at Croke Park, County Dublin

Championship and the Senior Hurling Championship. The original intention was that Croke should only host those traditional Gaelic sports that fell under the umbrella of the GAA. This has been the subject of contentious debate, and it was not until 2006 that it was agreed that rugby, a sport at which the Irish excel, and soccer could be played at the park, with the Six Nations rugby games and the soccer internationals played there during 2007.

However, it is the traditional games like hurling for which the GAA is famous. Hurling in some form or other dates back to pre-history and is the world's fastest field team sport. It is played using sticks called hurleys and a ball, referred to as a sliotar. The sliotar can be held in the hand for four paces, hit in the air, or hit on the ground using a hurley. It can also be kicked or slapped with an open hand, and balanced on the end of the hurley. Although the game has been in existence since pre-Christian times, the earliest written references date to the fifth century, and the game is even recorded as being played by some of Ireland's folklore heroes.

At the epicentre of Irish sport is Croke Park in Dublin, the largest sports stadium in Ireland. The park is famous for holding Gaelic sports competitions, including the ancient game of hurling, although it is also a popular venue for rock and pop concerts.

It is the home of the Gaelic Athletic Association (GAA), which was formed in 1884 and promotes Gaelic sports, as well as hosting Gaelic games such as the All-Ireland Senior Football

Gaelic Football

Tyrone vs. Armagh in a Gaelic football match

By the seventeenth century, the game had started to become popular amongst the wealthy as well as the lower classes, and gambling on the outcome of matches was prevalent. There have been attempts to ban Gaelic football along with hurling, but never with much success. It was not formalized until the nineteenth century when the GAA drew up a set of rules in 1884. The GAA set out to preserve the integrity of the game and to unify it, as well as making sure the rules made it markedly different from other sports such as soccer.

The game is played with two teams of fifteen players and lasts for 30 minutes each way at club level, or 35 minutes at inter-county level. The goal posts are similar to rugby goal posts, but with a lower cross bar. The ball is round and slightly smaller than a soccer ball, and can be carried for no more than four paces, before it must be dropped, bounced or kicked back into the hand. It can also be kicked or hand passed between players. Points are awarded for the ball being kicked or hand passed over the cross bar of the goal for one point, or under the cross bar and into the net for three points.

Gaelic Football enjoys a massive and dedicated following. Like hurling, Gaelic football is an ancient game that was doubtless played long before it was first documented, in 1308. Rather than an account of the game, this early record relates how a spectator at a match in Newcastle was charged with accidentally stabbing one of the players.

Gaelic football fans

Contemporary Music

Irish music has a long tradition and is an integral part of Irish culture. More recently, however, Ireland has also developed a reputation for hosting some of the largest rock bands in the world. Part of the attraction of Ireland as a centre for modern music concerts is her wealth of suitable venues, one of the more impressive of which is Slane Castle.

This imposing eighteenth-century castle can be found in the Boyne valley in the County of Meath, not far from the site of the famous Battle of the Boyne, 1690. Now instead of the clash of Irish, Scottish and English swords, the valley not infrequently rings with the sound of major rock bands, including Dublin's own superstars U2. The concerts are held annually and are staged in a naturally occurring amphitheatre, which can hold 100,000 music fans.

The province is home to a number of other concert venues. The annual rock festival, Oxegen, is held at the newly revamped Punchestown racecourse in County Kildare and attracts around 80,000 people a day. To the west of County Kildare is County Laois, and here at Stradbally Hall the annual Electric Picnic occurs. This three-day arts and music festival has featured alternative music artists such as Björk, Chemical Brothers and Sigur Rós.

Concert at Slane Castle, County Meath

Other venues include Malahide Castle, begun in the twelfth century and located 14 kms (9 miles) north of Dublin. Despite only opening as a rock venue in 2007, it has already hosted concerts by Arctic Monkeys, Pink, Joe Cocker and others, while Phoenix Park in Dublin has seen the likes of Coldplay, U2, Robbie Williams and Red Hot Chili Peppers grace its beautiful open-air space.

Agricultural Fairs

Agricultural fairs have a long, though often undocumented, history in Ireland. Today agricultural fairs and game fairs are widespread throughout the country, particularly across the province of Leinster, and are lively, entertaining and often educational events. Generally, agricultural fairs are held annually from the spring to September, and will most often combine livestock classes, machinery classes, displays of general rural interest, dog and horse shows, falconry and other countryside pursuits. As such they showcase almost every area of rural and agricultural life, and keep this important aspect of Irish life firmly in the public eye. Fairs such as this are family-friendly and geared towards children, encouraging them to participate in and learn about the countryside and farming matters. They also typically include many stalls selling local produce, foods, crafts, arts and various farming or livestock equipment. Most counties will hold their own 'county' fair, whilst other fairs may also be organised by separate associations or towns. There is also a National Irish County Show, which in 2009 will be held in the grounds of Ballinlough Castle in County Westmeath.

This exquisite building and its grounds are privately owned and have been in the same family for 400 years, providing the perfect backdrop to Ireland's most important agricultural fair.

Another fair, the Tinahely Agricultural Show, is held in the beautiful county of Wicklow at Fairwood Park, overlooking the surrounding Tomnafinogue Oak Wood. This fair is one of the largest of its kind and has been running since 1935, gradually expanding its classes and categories to cater for all ages and aspects of farming.

Agricultural Fair, Stradbally, County Laois

Agricultural Fair, Tinahely, County Wicklow

Revelers at the St Patrick's Day parade in Dublin

St Patrick's Day

There is possibly no more famous cultural association with Ireland than that of St Patrick (*c.* AD 387–461), the country's patron saint. St Patrick's Day is generally celebrated on March 17, and not only in Ireland, but also in many cities in Britain and the USA. However, one of the largest and most important centres for the celebration of the Emerald Isle's saint is Dublin, in the heart of Leinster. Every year a five-day festival is held, culminating in the famous St Patrick's Day parade, which is attended by upwards of 500,000 people.

The day has evolved to become a celebration of Ireland and Irish culture in all aspects, while adhering to its original Christian emphasis, although this is on occasion overshadowed by the fancy-dress green outfits and abundant food and drink. The Christian celebration, primarily in the Catholic and Church of Ireland churches, normally falls within the period of Lent. On occasion (1940 and 2008) March 17, St Patrick's Day has fallen during Holy Week, leading the holiday, rather contentiously, to be moved to a different date.

The colour green is frequently associated with Ireland and all things Irish, accounting for the prevalence of green seen during the festivities. This association may have come from the phrase 'the wearing of green', which refers to the custom of pinning a shamrock to clothing for luck. Interestingly, prior to the twentieth century, St Patrick was always associated with blue, and was frequently depicted in blue robes, to such an extent that there is a shade of blue known as St Patrick's Blue, and this is the colour that appears on the Irish Presidential Standard.

St Patrick's Day fireworks over the Customs House in Dublin
Next page: St Patrick's Day parade through Dublin

Dublin Festivals

Dublin truly is the jewel in the crown of Leinster. Not only is she full of history and stunning architectural monuments, but she is also the heart of many of Ireland's cultural traditions, being a focal point for arts, culture, music, literature and dance festivals. Dublin has a diverse and full programme of festivals, which occur all year round and attract a wide cross-section of people. She enjoys a booming tourist industry and is possibly Ireland's most vivacious and cosmopolitan city.

Different festivals celebrate all of Ireland's cultural traditions, from the annual Guinness Blues Festival held over the third weekend of July, to the two-week Dublin Fringe Festival, which is Ireland's largest-growing festival that promotes new and established performing artists. The vibrant May Day parade is held on the first day of May, and traces its roots back to pagan ritual and the celebration of the end of winter in the northern hemisphere. It features dancers in traditional dress and bright costumes, and still retains its pagan roots, despite it more recently being aligned with the American International Worker's Day to represent the rights and struggles of workers. Also in the spring is the Dublin Dance Festival that promotes Irish talent as well as welcoming international acts, and the Bloom Festival, situated in Dublin's magnificent Phoenix Park, the most spectacular gardening and flower event in Ireland.

Street theatre in the Temple Bar area as part of the Guinness Blues Festival

May Day parade though Dublin

Theatre & Literature in Dublin

Dublin has given birth to both famous actors and literary giants. Among them is James Joyce (1882–1941), who based his celebrated work *Ulysses* in Dublin. Today June 16 is recognised as Bloomsbury Day, the day in 1904 on which all the action of *Ulysses* takes place. The revelry often lasts for up to a week with admirers of Joyce travelling from all over the world to take part.

Other famous literary figures to hail from the city include Oscar Wilde (1854–1900), Bram Stoker (1847–1912), Jonathan Swift (1667–1745) and George Bernard Shaw (1856–1950). Dublin is also home to Ireland's National Library, and the National Print Museum of Ireland.

Within the centre of Dublin is a cluster of famous theatres of which The Abbey, or National Theatre of Ireland, is particularly interesting. The original theatre was founded in 1904, but was destroyed in a fire in 1951, and rebuilt on Lower Abbey Street. It was the first theatre in the United Kingdom and Ireland to be partially funded by state subsidy, and was originally set up by a group of literary figures that included William Butler Yeats (1865–1939), specifically to promote Irish literary and theatrical talent.

Another of Dublin's famous theatres is the colourful Olympia, which was opened in 1897 on the site of an old music hall. The theatre stayed open until 1974, when part of the interior collapsed during a break in rehearsals for *West Side Story*. The building was closed for restoration and opened again in 1977. The Gaiety Theatre is also a historic gem, and was opened in 1871 on South King Street. The theatre is host mostly to musicals, dance and operatic productions, with possibly its most famous event being the Christmas pantomime, which has run for many years.

Man in costume on Bloomsbury Day

Guinness

The thick and creamy stout Guinness is one of Ireland's most famous and best-loved exports. It is synonymous with the Irish, an important part of their culture and enjoyed across the world, with an estimated ten million pints of Guinness drunk every day. Dublin is the home of Guinness, and it was here that Arthur Guinness leased the St James's Gate Brewery in 1759, where he developed the powerful stout. Arthur learnt the brewing trade from his father, and first started brewing ale at St James's Gate, before developing a dark stout called Porter during the 1770s. Porter quickly became a firm favourite with imbibers, and by 1799 Arthur had ceased to brew ale completely and devoted his energies to Porter and developing beers and stouts.

Arthur's son, Arthur Guinness II, took over the brewery in 1803 and expanded the export business. By the 1830s the family-run company was the largest brewery in Ireland. Arthur II's son, Benjamin Lee Guinness, took over in 1855 and quickly created the trade-mark name Guinness. In turn, his son Edward Cecil headed up the company from 1868, turning it into the largest brewery in the world. By the end of the nineteenth century the original four-acre site had grown to over 60 acres.

The company did not actually begin an advertising campaign until 1929, and followed this with the launch of new products including Guinness Draught in 1959. Possibly the most innovative and famous Guinness development was that of canned Guinness Draught in 1988, which was based on the use of breakthrough technology in packaging, namely the 'widget'.

Guinness Brewery, St James's Gate

Beef & Guinness Casserole

SERVES 4

INGREDIENTS

2 tbsp olive oil

900g/2lbs/5 cups stewing beef, such as rib steak or shoulder, cut into thin slices

1 onion, chopped

2 leeks, sliced

2 carrots, sliced

2 celery sticks, sliced

2 garlic cloves, finely chopped

300ml/½ pint/1¼ cups well-reduced beef stock

150ml/¼ pint/⅔ cup Guinness

50g/2oz/¼ cup butter

75g/3oz/⅓ cup streaky/fatty bacon, trimmed and diced

115g/4oz/1¼ cups wild or cultivated mushrooms, quartered or sliced

50g/2oz/½ cup shallots or small onions, left whole

25g/1oz/¼ cup plain/all-purpose flour

salt and ground black pepper

1 Heat the oil in a pan and brown the meat. Transfer to a casserole. Sauté the vegetables for 5 minutes in the pan.

2 Add the vegetables to the meat with the garlic, the stock and the Guinness. Season. Cover the casserole and bring to the boil, then reduce the heat and simmer for about 1½ hours.

3 Remove the meat from the casserole and strain the cooking liquid and reserve. Discard the vegetables.

4 Clean the casserole and sauté the bacon, mushrooms and shallots or onions in the butter for 5–10 minutes. When the vegetables are tender, sprinkle in the flour and cook, stirring, over a low heat for 2–3 minutes, then slowly blend in the reserved cooking liquid. Return the meat to the casserole, and reheat. Serve with mashed potatoes.

ORIGINS AND TRADITIONS

Guinness has been brewed in Dublin since 1759. When used in cooking it helps to tenderize the meat and adds its rich, malty flavour to any dish.

Dublin Coddle

MAKES 4 LARGE OR 8 SMALL PORTIONS

INGREDIENTS

8 x 8mm/⅓in thick ham or dry-cured bacon slices
8 best-quality lean pork sausages
4 large onions, thinly sliced
900g/2 lbs/5 cups potatoes, peeled and sliced
6 tbsp chopped fresh parsley
salt and ground black pepper

1 Cut the ham or bacon into large chunks and cook with the sausages in 1.2 ltrs/2 pts/5 cups boiling water for 5 minutes. Drain, but reserve the cooking liquor.

2 Put the meat into a pan or ovenproof dish with the onions, potatoes and the parsley. Season, and add just enough of the reserved cooking liquor to cover. Cover with a tight-fitting lid; lay a piece of buttered foil or baking parchment on top before putting on the lid.

3 Simmer gently over a low heat for about 1 hour, or until the liquid is reduced by half and all the ingredients are cooked but not mushy. Serve hot with the vegetables on top with the traditional accompaniments of fresh soda bread and a glass of stout.

ORIGINS AND TRADITIONS

Coddle was reputedly a favourite dish of Jonathan Swift, author of *Gulliver's Travels* and Dean of St. Patrick's Cathedral in Dublin.

Dublin Lawyer

SERVES 2

INGREDIENTS

1 large, (over 900g/2lb) lightly cooked lobster
175g/6oz/¾ cup butter
75ml/2½fl oz/⅓ cup Irish whiskey
150ml/¼ pint/⅔ cup double/heavy cream
sea salt and ground black pepper

1 To cook the lobster, weigh it and put it into a pan of boiling salted water. Bring back to the boil and cook for 12 minutes per 450g/1lb for small lobsters, a little less if 900g/2lb or over. Remove the cooked lobster from the water and leave to cool.

2 Tear off the claws from the cooked lobster. Split the body in half lengthways, with a sharp knife, just slightly to the right of the centre line to avoid cutting into the digestive

tract. Remove the grey matter from the head of the shell and discard. Remove the digestive tract right down the length of the body and discard. Lift the flesh from the tail – it usually comes out in one piece. Set the shells aside for serving and keep them warm.

3 Tear the two joints in the claw to separate them and, using a small knife, scoop out the flesh. With the back of a heavy knife, hit the claw near the pincers, rotating the claw and hitting until the claw opens. Remove the flesh and cut into bitesize pieces.

4 Melt the butter in a pan over a low heat. Add the lobster pieces and turn in the butter to warm through. Warm the whiskey in a separate pan and pour it over the lobster. Carefully set it alight. Add the cream and heat gently without allowing the sauce to boil, then season to taste. Turn the hot mixture into the warm shells and serve immediately.

ORIGINS AND TRADITIONS

Although no one is sure where Dublin Lawyer got its name, local folklore is that it is because Dublin lawyers had a reputation for being rich and drinking a lot of whiskey.

Gur Cake

INGREDIENTS

8 slices stale bread, or plain cake

75g/3oz/⅔ cup plain/all-purpose flour

pinch of salt

½ tsp baking powder

2 tsp mixed/apple pie spice

115g/4oz/generous ½ cup granulated sugar, plus extra for
  sprinkling

175g/6oz/¾ cup currants or mixed dried fruit

50g/2oz/¼ cup butter, melted

1 egg, lightly beaten

milk to mix

FOR THE SHORTCRUST PASTRY:

225g/8oz/2 cups
  plain/all-purpose flour

½ tsp salt

115g/4oz/½ cup butter

ORIGINS AND TRADITIONS

Gur Cake was an invention of Dublin bakers early in the
twentieth century as a way to use up day-old bread or cake.

1   To make the shortcrust pastry dough, mix together the
flour, salt and the butter in a large mixing bowl. Using the
fingertips or a pastry/cookie cutter, rub the butter into the
flour until the mixture resembles fine breadcrumbs.

2   Mix in 2–3 tbsp cold water and knead the mixture lightly
to form a firm dough. Wrap the dough in clingfilm/plastic
wrap and chill in the refrigerator for 30 minutes.

3   Preheat the oven to 190°C/375°F/Gas 5 and grease and
flour a square baking tin/pan.

4   Remove the crusts from the bread and make the remainder
into crumbs, or make the cake into crumbs. Put the crumbs
into a mixing bowl with the flour, salt, baking powder, mixed/
apple pie spice, sugar and dried fruit. Mix well to combine.

5   Add the butter and egg to the dry ingredients with enough
milk to make a fairly stiff, spreadable mixture.

6   Roll out the pastry dough and, using the baking tin/pan as a
guide, cut out one piece to make the lid. Use the rest, re-rolled
as necessary, to line the base of the tin/pan. Spread the bottom
layer of pastry with the mixture then cover with the pastry lid.

7   Make diagonal slashes across the top. Bake in the oven for
50–60 minutes, or until golden. Sprinkle with sugar and
leave to cool in the tin/pan. Cut into slices.

Munster

Landscapes

THE DELIGHTFUL province of Munster is the most southerly and largest of Ireland's four provinces and is made up of six counties – Cork, Kerry, Clare, Tipperary, Limerick and Waterford. It is overwhelmingly beautiful and is a province defined by its rural heart and natural splendour. The area's largest towns are: Waterford City, situated on the east coast and famous for its glass-making (the factory tragically went into receivership on 5 January 2009); Cork City in the south of the province, with the largest natural harbour in Europe; and Limerick City on the west coast, an important centre of industry, and home to King John's Castle, built on a former Viking settlement.

Lush, green hills and pastures crossed by the rivers Bandon, Blackwater, Lee, Shannon and Suir roll down towards the picturesque and scenic coastline, of which the area around west Cork is particularly stunning. This includes Ballybrannigan Beach that becomes quite magical as the sun sets. Munster's rocky coastline is dotted with small fishing villages, natural harbours and hidden coves, while at the most western point of Munster in County Kerry is the extraordinary Dingle Peninsula. Just inland and affording spectacular views across the area is Mount Brandon. County Kerry also boasts the 'Ring of Kerry', a 170-km (106-mile) circular road that takes in many of the area's most impressive sites, including Skellig Michael and the Killarney National Park.

One of the most famous sites in Munster is the Blarney Stone, built into the battlements of the mediaeval Blarney Castle near Cork. According to legend, those who kiss the stone become blessed with 'the gift of the gab', a trait associated with the Irish people.

Bantry House and Gardens, County Cork

Tipperary & Cork Landmarks

The land-locked county of Tipperary is amongst the most fertile in Ireland and is home to the 'Golden Vale', a rich and productive area of land in the basin of the River Suir that runs north/south through the county. To the south and west of Tipperary are mountain ranges, and the north borders the magnificent Lough Derg. Across this beautiful region is scattered a wealth of historic sites and natural wonders, including the Glen of Aherlow valley, the enormous twelfth-century Cahir Castle and the Rock of Cashel to name just a few. Of these the Rock of Cashel is amongst the most impressive with its collection of buildings dating from the twelfth century. The rocky outcrop was settled before this date, and is reputed to have been the seat of Munster's kings, although no structures survive from this period. Legend recounts that it was here that St Patrick converted the King of Munster to Christianity in the fifth century AD.

To the south of Tipperary lies Cork, which is an area of unsurpassed beauty crossed by deep glacial valleys, with soft-green hills and a picturesque coastline. Cork County has one of the smallest populations, with a high proportion of the population based around her largest conurbation, Cork City. Consequently, the rest of the county remains thoroughly unspoilt, quiet and sparsely populated. Not far from Cork City, and to the north-west, is Blarney Castle, famous for the Blarney Stone, and originally dating to before 1200. Another architectural gem is Bantry House, situated on the south side of Bantry Bay in the west of County Cork. The house was built in 1700 and is set in stunning terraced and landscaped gardens.

Blarney Castle, County Cork   Next Page: Rock of Cashel, County Tipperary

Coastal Cork

The County of Cork wears her lovely, rugged coastline like a diadem of jewels, and it is with little doubt one of the most beautiful stretches of coastline in the country. It has a wild and untamed beauty and a drama all of its own. Wild flowers grow in abundance along the irregular coastline in the spring and summer, and narrow winding roads offer surprising, sudden views across to the Atlantic before meandering their way into the many small fishing villages. These charming and quaint villages, of which Allihies is one, are quite distinctive through their brightly coloured houses, which string along the coastline in a range of cheerful hues. Allihies can be found on the Béara Peninsula, and was a centre of copper mining until the 1870s. The peninsula falls between Kenmore Bay and Bantry Bay, and is home to the haunting ruins of Dunboy Castle and its neighbour, the nineteenth-century Puxley Castle which was burnt to the ground by the IRA in 1920. The 'Ring of Béara' is a 195-km (121-mile) road route around the peninsula taking in some of its most beautiful sites.

The coast of Cork boasts what is reputed to be the world's second largest natural harbour on its east side below the border with County Waterford. The harbour is so big that numerous towns are to be found along its perimeter, including Cork City, and it encompasses a number of islands including Great Island, which sits at the mouth of the River Lee where it joins the sea, and the smaller Fota Island. Fota Island has Ireland's only wildlife park as well as the magnificent, eighteenth-century Fota House.

Ballybrannigan Beach

County Kerry

The magnificent County Kerry, sometimes referred to as 'the Kingdom', can be roughly divided into two areas based on its terrain. The north of the county is covered with smooth, rolling hills and lush pastures that lead gently down to pristine, sandy beaches, while the south and west are defined by rugged, mountainous scenery, ancient historic sites and flat, glassy lakes. The coastline also boasts the Dingle Peninsula in the north, on which can be found many sites of interest, including the Gallarus Oratory, the only surviving boat-shaped oratory in Ireland, dating back to the eighth century AD.

Below the Dingle Peninsula is the Iveragh Peninsula, which is the largest peninsula in south-west Ireland. Stretching down the centre of the peninsula is the Macgillycuddy's Reeks mountain range, which includes the highest peak, Carrauntoohil, in Ireland. At the foot of the mountains lie the lakes of Killarney, surrounded by woodland, rivers and dramatic waterfalls. This area is Killarney National Park, the first national park to be set up in Ireland when it was donated by the Muckross estate to the nation in 1932. Within the park is Muckross House, a splendid nineteeth-century mansion built by the Scottish architect William Burn (1789–1870).

Ogham Stone at Dunmore Head, Dingle Peninsula

Around 12 kms (7 miles) from the west coast of the Iveragh Peninsula are two small but forbidding islands. Little Skellig is closed to the public and is an important breeding ground for gannets. Great Skellig, or Skellig Michael, holds the ruins of a 600-year-old monastery, which clings to the sheer cliffs of the island. This most desolate place is a stark reminder of the unwavering devotion and conviction of the monks who lived there.

County Clare

Lying in the north-west corner of Munster is County Clare, which contains the limestone plain referred to as the Burren. It could be said to be a county of water and rock, bordering the enormous Lough Derg, the third largest lake in Ireland, in the north-east, the great River Shannon in the south-east, and giving way to the Atlantic Ocean in the west. The Burren, a wild land of rock and ancient history, covers over 160 sq km (100 sq miles) of her interior, and plunging cliff-faces such as the impressive Cliffs of Moher form much of her coastline, interspersed with sweeping, sandy beaches. Nearby O'Brien's Tower, built in 1835 by Sir Cornelius O'Brien (1782–1857), on a clear day offers views across to the Aran Islands in Galway Bay.

Cliffs of Moher

The principal town in the county is Ennis, which lies along the River Fergus and has a thriving music culture, particularly traditional music. Not far from the town is Bunratty Castle, built on a settlement established in around AD 970. The castle has had a chequered history, having been built, destroyed and rebuilt several times, with the present structure dating to the fifteenth century. From Ennis and travelling westwards, Clare opens into the West Clare Peninsula, at the end of which is Loop Head with its lonely lighthouse. This is a spot slightly off the beaten tourist trail, but is staggeringly beautiful and well worth a visit.

The Burren

In the north-west of County Clare stretches an extraordinary piece of rocky landscape over 100 acres in size made up of rocky hills, cliffs, gorges, caves, tunnels and sea cliffs. To the west the Burren is bounded by the Atlantic and to the north by the majestic Galway Bay. The area is made up of layers of limestone, many of which appear much like giant paving slabs. The landscape supports a diverse and abundant range of flora and fauna, including, rather unusually, Mediterranean, Arctic and Alpine types of plants growing side by side.

Across the dramatic lands of the Burren there is noticeable evidence of its ancient past, which includes over 90 megalithic tombs and portal dolmens. One of the most impressive, dating to between 4200 BC and 2900 BC, is the Poulnabrone Dolmen, which translates as 'hole of sorrows'. Excavations here discovered the remains of at least 22 people. Around one kilometre south is the well-preserved Caherconnell Stone Fort, which is a Celtic ring fort that dates to approximately 500 BC and is thought to have been inhabited into the Middle Ages.

Other sites of interest include a Celtic High Cross, which can be found in the village of Kilfenora to the south of the Burren, and the thirteenth-century Cistercian Corcomroe

Poulnabrone Dolmen, County Clare

Abbey, which is located to the north. The abbey contains examples of quite spectacular carving and ornament, rare for their date. One of the Burren's most dramatic natural wonders is the Aillwee Cave with its underground river and waterfall, which is just part of the network of caves that run beneath the limestone ground.

Culture

MUNSTER is an area with a strong arts and crafts tradition, of which Waterford glass in County Waterford and Kenmore lacemaking in County Kerry are amongst the most famous examples, tracing their respective histories back to the eighteenth and nineteenth centuries. Munster is home to some of Ireland's most prestigious artistic institutions, including The National Self-Portrait Collection and the Limerick City Museum and Gallery of Art in Limerick, and the Crawford Gallery and Lewis Glucksman Gallery in Cork. The province is noted for its rich collection of early Celtic art treasures, such as the exquisite Ardagh Chalice found in County Limerick and the Petrie Crown, discovered in County Cork, both now housed in the National Museum of Ireland in Dublin.

Music too forms an important part of Munster's character, with towns like Ennis, County Clare, hosting many musical events. Possibly most redolent of Munster's rich traditions is the eclectic Puck Fair in Killorglin, County Kerry, which evokes the magical heart of Ireland through music and dance.

Festivals are popular and widespread throughout Munster, including agricultural fairs, arts, food and music festivals, that both entertain and keep the old traditions alive. The village of Ballydehob in County Cork holds a number of festivals including the colourful religious Corpus Christi, and has the honour of having more pubs per capita than any other town in Ireland – pubs too can be considered part of Ireland's culture!

Munster also plays host to professional and recreational sporting activities. Some of the finest golf courses in Ireland are found here, along with virtually every recreational activity from potholing to sailing, and riding to hill walking. The province has strong affiliations with hurling and Gaelic football, with County Kerry having produced the most successful football team in the history of the game.

Munster Sport

Ballybunion Golf Course, County Kerry

The 'greens' of County Clare and County Kerry in particular are popular with golfers; Kerry's Ballybunion Golf Course is widely regarded as being one of the top-ten courses in the world. Kerry is also a favourite haunt of anglers, both inland and sea anglers, with the River Laune in mid to south-west Kerry boasting excellent salmon fishing set amongst idyllic scenery.

Munster has a long tradition of watersports: the world's oldest yacht club is based at Crosshaven, a village that sits in Cork's enormous natural harbour, while the coastline of County Clare boasts many sailing centres. Lough Derg in the east of the county provides many watersports and boating facilities, and in Limerick to the south the River Shannon is used for both fishing and water activities.

The diverse nature of Munster's landscape, ranging from rolling hills to vertiginous cliffs and craggy mountains, and her abundance of water make her a sought-after destination for sporting enthusiasts. Virtually every type of recreational sporting activity is catered for within her six counties, which includes spectator sports such as greyhound and horse racing in County Limerick and Gaelic football, hurling and Camogie in County Tipperary and County Limerick.

The beautiful and at times dramatic scenery across the province make walking and horse riding top activities. Horse riding is fairly consistently available throughout Ireland, but the landscape of Munster lends an added draw for equestrian enthusiasts.

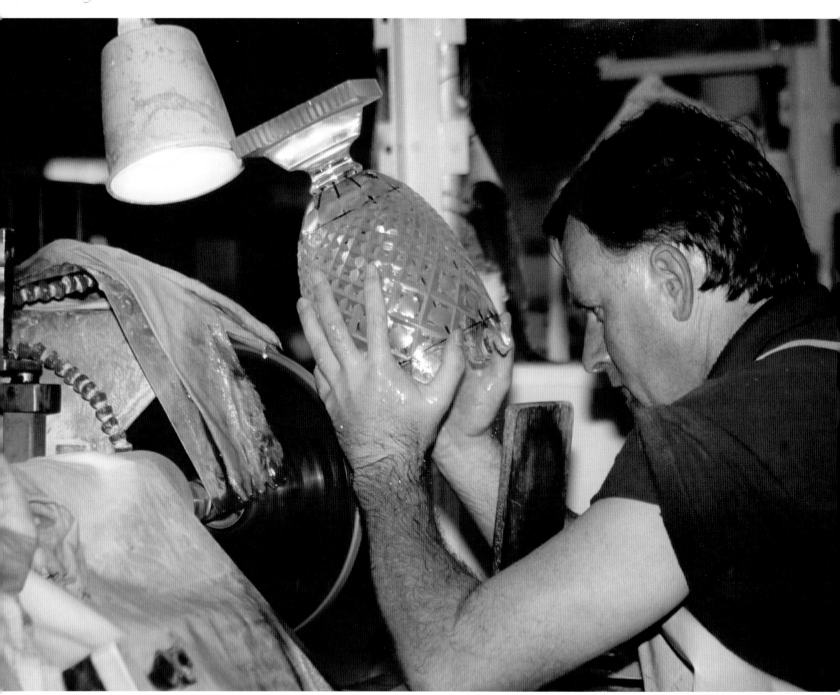

Munster Arts & Crafts

The tradition of arts and crafts in Munster includes fine art, sculpture and traditional crafts. Some of Ireland's most prestigious art galleries can be found in the province, including the Hunt Museum in Limerick, which has one of the largest private collections of arts and artefacts in Ireland, and the Waterford Art Gallery. Other major galleries are the National Self-Portrait Collection, Limerick, which houses over 400 works by native or resident Irish artists, the modern Lewis Glucksman Gallery in Cork and the Limerick City Museum and Gallery of Art.

Munster is probably best known for her Waterford crystal glassware and Kenmore lace. The first crystal glassware business opened in Waterford City in 1783 and lasted for around twenty years. It was long enough to establish the city's reputation as a leading producer of the highest-quality glassware, much of which had found its way into the homes of royalty across Europe. Another glass industry was set up in 1947 before being taken over by the Irish Bottle Company. Waterford Crystal later became a subsiduary of Waterford Wedgewood plc, and Waterford Crystal remains a popular and traditional gift to royalty and travelling heads of state.

Kenmore Lace was established in the town of Kenmore, County Clare by nuns who travelled to the area in 1861.

It was a time of great poverty for locals who had been blighted by the potato famine of 1845–51. The nuns developed a lace-making industry and taught its art to the locals. Part of the appeal of Irish lace is the intricate and beautiful designs, many of which were closely guarded family secrets. A school of design was established in Kenmore with affiliations with the Kensington College of Art in London and the Crawford School of Art in Cork.

Handmade lace, Kenmore, County Clare

Irish Pubs

Ireland is famed for her pubs, poor imitations of which have appeared across the world, and it is true to say that nowhere are pubs quite like those found on the Emerald Isle. Pub culture is not confined to Munster, but Ballydehob in County Cork is a small village that boasts the most pubs per capita in the country. Every town and village has their pubs, which are more than simple 'watering holes' and form the heart and soul of the area, serving as social hubs and business forums: it is many a fine deal that has been struck in the local pub!

Beer was originally brewed in the home and was a mainstay of the diet, particularly in areas where the water was polluted. Surplus would be sold off to neighbours, which led to the concept of brewing being linked with income. These home-brew establishments became basic beer shops, places where clients would buy beer, and occasionally stop a while for a chat and a drink. So began the evolution of the 'pub'.

Irish pubs are particularly noted for their attractive and rustic appeal, often with wood bars, simple furnishings and, in more rural locations, brightly coloured doors. Pub signs have also become greatly decorated and virtual works of art, but this was not always the case. Originaly Irish pub signs would just have borne the name of the landlord, or their coat of arms. The rural

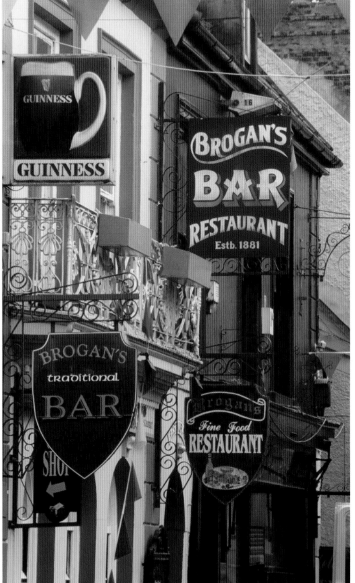

O'Connell Street, Ennis, County Clare

community would have been largely illiterate, so symbols and pictures were used. This tradition of clear symbols and pictures on pub signs is still very much in evidence today.

Munster Festivals & Fairs

Munster has a long tradition of festivals and fairs that celebrate a diverse range of rural and contemporary life, from the arts to agriculture. Virtually every Munster town holds a variety of fairs and festivals, which promote traditional cultures and are a great excuse for a 'knees up'. Tourists travel from far and wide to experience the very unique flavour of Irish festivals, particularly noted for their friendly ambience where all who attend are welcomed with open arms.

While these festivals serve a commercial purpose, they also, possibly more importantly, help to keep the old traditions alive. There is no better showcase for this than the annual Steam and Vintage Rally at Innishannon, County Cork, which holds exhibitions and classes for vintage tractors, steam engines, oil engines, cars and even threshers. Of a slightly different nature is the three-day Bantry Mussel Fair in Bantry, Country Cork with free mussels available at local bars.

Steam and Vintage Rally, Innishannon, County Cork

Music has played a central part in Irish cultural life, and the high number of music festivals in the province and elsewhere reflects this. Notable amongst these are the Shindig Arts and Culture Festival in Tralee, County Kerry, the Rosscarbery Arts and Literature Fair, Rosscarbery, County Cork and the Féile na nDéise traditional music festival at Dungarvan, County Waterford. Ballydehob, a small town in County Cork, in addition to the Ballydehob Jazz Festival, boasts a strong and varied schedule of festivals including the colourful religious festival of Corpus Christi, a Threshing and Vintage Festival and annual road trotting races.

KING PUCK

Puck Fair

There are few fairs or festivals that celebrate the goat, but the Puck Fair in Killorglin, Country Kerry, does just that. The origins of the fair are shrouded in mystery, although it is believed to date to pre-Christian times. The high point of the fair is the crowning of King Puck, a local goat who is deemed worthy, and each year a young girl is crowned Queen Puck. It is possible that the goat was seen as a pagan figure of fertility, and lines can be drawn between this and the ancient Greek, half-goat and half-man god of fertility, Pan. The first record of the fair was in 1603, and then in a charter when King James I granted it legal status.

Another popular story surrounding the lauding of the goat dates to the time of Oliver Cromwell (1599–1658). The story recounts that while the English troops were rampaging through the countryside, they disturbed a herd of goats at the foot of the Macgillycuddy's Reeks. The animals scattered into the foothills with the exception of one billy goat who headed to the town of Killorglin. His arrival there, exhausted and frightened, alerted the townsfolk to the impending danger, and they were able to prepare themselves for the oncoming soldiers. In honour of the goat, the people dedicated their fair to him, and it has been held ever since.

Bagpipe performance at Puck Fair, Killorglin, County Kerry

The fair is held annually on 10, 11 and 12 August, and includes a horse fair, traditional music, arts and crafts, parades, the crowning of the King Puck and Queen Puck, circus acts and many other lively activities.

Dingle Pies

MAKES 6
SMALL PIES

INGREDIENTS

450g/1lb boneless mutton or lamb

1 large onion, diced

2 carrots, diced

1 potato, diced

2 celery sticks, diced

1 egg, beaten

salt and ground black pepper

FOR THE SHORTCRUST PASTRY:

500g/1¼lb/5 cups plain/all-purpose flour

250g/9oz/generous 1 cup butter, or half butter and half
  white vegetable fat/shortening

120ml/4fl oz/½ cup very cold water

1 To make the pastry dough, sieve the flour into a large bowl
and add the butter. Rub the butter into the flour with the
fingertips or a pastry blender, lifting the mixture as much as
possible to aerate. Add the chilled water. Mix with a knife
or fork until the mixture clings together. Turn it onto a
floured worktop and knead lightly once or twice until
smooth. Wrap in baking parchment or foil and leave in the
refrigerator to relax for 20 minutes before using.

2 Trim any fat or gristle from the meat and cut it up into
very small pieces. Place in a large bowl and add the diced
onion, carrots, potato and celery. Mix well and season with
salt and freshly ground black pepper.

3 Preheat the oven to 180°C/350°F/Gas 4. Cut a third off
the ball of pastry dough and reserve to make the lids of the
pies. Roll out the rest and, using a small plate as a guide
and re-rolling the pastry dough as necessary, cut out six
circles. Divide the meat and vegetable mixture between the
circles, piling it in the middle of each.

4 Roll out the remaining pastry dough and cut out six
smaller circles, about 10cm/4in across. Lay these on top.
Dampen the edges of the pastry bases, bring the pastry
dough up around the meat, pleat it to fit the lid and pinch
the edges together.

5 Make a small hole in the top of each pie to let out the
steam, brush them with beaten egg and slide the pies on to
baking sheets. Bake in the preheated oven for an hour.
Serve hot or cold.

ORIGINS AND TRADITIONS

Dingle pies were, and still are, sold at traditional and
agricultural fairs. They could easily be bought from a stall
and carried around while you had a look at the cattle or
met with old friends.

Spiced Beef

SERVES 8

INGREDIENTS

1 tbsp coarsely ground black pepper

2 tsp ground ginger

1 tbsp juniper berries, crushed

1 tbsp coriander seeds, crushed

1 tsp ground cloves

1 tbsp ground allspice

3 tbsp soft dark brown sugar

2 bay leaves, crushed

1 small onion, finely chopped

1.8 kg/4lb corned beef, silverside or tail end

300 ml/½ pint/1¼ cups Guinness

fruit chutney and bread, to serve

1 First, spice the beef: blend the pepper, spices and sugar thoroughly, then mix in the bay leaves and onion. Rub the mixture into the meat, then put it into a suitable lidded container and refrigerate for 3–4 days, turning and rubbing with the mixture daily.

2 Put the meat into a pan and barely cover with cold water. Place a tight lid on the pan and bring to a boil. Reduce the heat and cook very gently for about 3½ hours. For the last hour add the Guinness to the cooking liquid.

3 When the joint is cooked, leave it to cool in the liquid. Wrap in foil and keep in the refrigerator until required. It will keep for about 1 week.

4 Serve on thinly sliced brown bread with chutney.

ORIGINS AND TRADITIONS

Spiced Beef is traditionally eaten at Christmas time when it can be found in almost every Irish butcher's window, often with a red ribbon tied around it.

Colcannon

SERVES 4

INGREDIENTS

450 g/1 lb/½ a cabbage

450 g/1 lb/2½ cups potatoes

2 leeks

250 ml/8 fl oz/1 cup milk

salt and black pepper, to taste

125 g/4 oz/½ butter, melted

1 In a large saucepan boil the cabbage until tender. Remove and chop or blend well. Set aside and keep warm.

2 Boil the potatoes until tender. Remove from the heat and drain.

3 Chop the leeks into rounds, the green parts as well as the white. Place them in a pan and pour in enough milk just to cover them. Simmer until the leeks are soft.

4 Season and mash the potatoes well. Stir in the cooked leeks and milk. Blend in the majority of the cabbage, then heat until the whole mixture is pale green and has a fluffy consistency. Garnish with the remaining cabbage and serve.

ORIGINS AND TRADITIONS

An old Irish Halloween tradition was to serve colcannon with small coins concealed within it.

Barm Brack

SERVES 12

INGREDIENTS

400 g/14 oz/2⅔ cups chopped dried mixed fruit

350 ml/12 fl oz/1½ cups hot brewed tea

300 g/10 oz/2½ cups plain/all-purpose flour

1 tsp ground cinnamon

1 tsp ground nutmeg

1 tsp bicarbonate of/baking soda

1 egg

300 g/10 oz/1½ cups sugar

80 g/3 oz/½ cup lemon marmalade

1 tsp grated orange zest

1 Soak the dried fruit in the hot tea for 2 hours, then drain and gently squeeze out excess tea.

2 Preheat oven to 175°C/350°F/Gas Mark 4. Grease an 18 cm/7 inch round baking tin. Stir together the flour, cinnamon, nutmeg, and bicarbonate of/baking soda. Set aside.

3 Beat the egg, sugar, marmalade, orange zest, and tea-soaked fruit until well combined. Gently fold in the flour until just combined, then pour into the prepared baking tin/pan.

4 Bake in the preheated oven for 1 hour or until the top of the cake springs back when lightly pressed. Allow to cool in the tin/pan for 2 hours before removing. Continue to cool to room temperature on a wire rack.

ORIGINS AND TRADITIONS

Traditionally made at Halloween, charms were baked inside the Barm Brack that were thought to predict the fortunes of those who found them. For example, a piece of cloth was a warning of bad luck or poverty, whereas a ring signified marriage.

Connacht

Landscapes

CONNACHT is the most westerly of Ireland's provinces and has some of her wildest landscapes. It has the lowest population of Ireland's four provinces and consists of just five counties – Galway, Leitrim, Roscommon, Mayo and Sligo. Gaelic heritage and traditions are perhaps best preserved here and the Irish language is still spoken in certain areas. These areas are collectively known as the Gaeltacht, which includes the rugged Aran Islands situated 14 kms (9 miles) off the coast of Galway.

The largest of the three Aran Islands is Inishmore, the site of the extraordinary pre-historic Dun Aengus Fort. The fort dates to around 700 BC and clings to the vertiginous western cliffs of the island. All three of the Aran Islands are home to an abundant variety of wildlife and offer quite spectacular scenery. Connacht as an area is truly defined by its landscapes. County Galway, the second largest county in Ireland, is divided in two by the magnificent Lough Corrib. To the west lies Connemara, with her mountainous regions and haunting bog lands, her famous native ponies and wild coastline dotted with cottages and churches. To the east of the lough the land opens into rich and fertile pastures, which roll into Mayo County.

To the north of Connacht is County Sligo, made famous by William Butler Yeats' (1865–1939) affectionate descriptions. Here the great, loaf-shaped Ben Bulben rises, providing panoramic views across the county. The pre-history of the area is much in evidence, with sites like the Stone Age cemetery at Carrowmore, west of Sligo town, and the tomb of Queen Meabh, the legendary queen of Connacht, on Knocknarea Mountain.

Aran Islands

The Aran Islands are made up of three islands, the largest being Inishmore. They can be found in the mouth of the spectacular Galway Bay, approximately 14 km (9 miles) off the coast. The islands are geologically similar to the rocky landscape of the Burren in County Clare in Munster, and have an extraordinarily wild and untamed beauty. They are littered with the evidence of their ancient past, particularly Inishmore where the impressive Iron Age fort of Dun Aengus can be found perched on the cliff edge. The fort is defensively surrounded by three concentric rings of stone, and in between the outer and middle walls is an area of thousands of jagged rock pillars, with a narrow diagonal path leading through them.

To the south-east of Inishmore is the island of Inishmaan, which is only 5 km (3 miles) long and 3 km (2 miles) wide. Though little, this island boasts wonderful scenery, the noted oval pre-Christian fort, Dun Couchubhuir, and the unusual rectangular fourth-century AD fort of Dun Fearbhaí.

The most eastern island is the tiny Inisheer, which at around 3 sq km (2 sq miles) is also the smallest. Inisheer is a haven for wildlife, and a walker's paradise. The mediaeval O'Brien's Castle can be found in the middle of the island as well as a scattering of tiny churches. One of the most interesting is Teampall

Inisheer, County Galway

Chaomháin, a tenth-century church on the beach, which periodically has to have the sand dug away from it to prevent it being buried.

Coastal Galway

The plunging Atlantic Ocean has shaped the coast of Galway into a myriad of small coves, steep cliffs and picturesque beaches. The waves crash onto the shoreline on this most westerly part of Ireland with relentless ferocity, and have created some of the most interesting and spectacular coastal scenery to be found in Ireland. Part of the charm of much of Ireland, and this region in particular, is its untamed nature, and this extends through the raw geology of the landscape to the relative isolation of her lands, and the abundant wildlife. It is not unusual here to stumble across donkeys roaming seemingly free, or herds of the famous Connemara ponies, both of which are intrinsically linked to Ireland's history and heritage.

Ireland is famous for her seafood and salmon, and the coast of Galway is a prime area associated with this industry. Many fishing villages dot the coastline such as Rossaveal, 36 km (22 miles) west of Galway City and famous for its seafood production. Mannin Bay just outside Clifden in the north of the county is famed for its organic salmon and for its breathtaking sandy beaches. Just to the west of Clifden is the Sky Road, a fascinating 11-km (7-mile) drive that follows the coastline, passing such sites as the crumbling Gothic Clifden Castle (a short walk from the road) and the ruins of the old coastguard station, and offering views of the dramatic Twelve Bens, a small but impressive mountain range with wonderful walking trails.

Mannin Bay

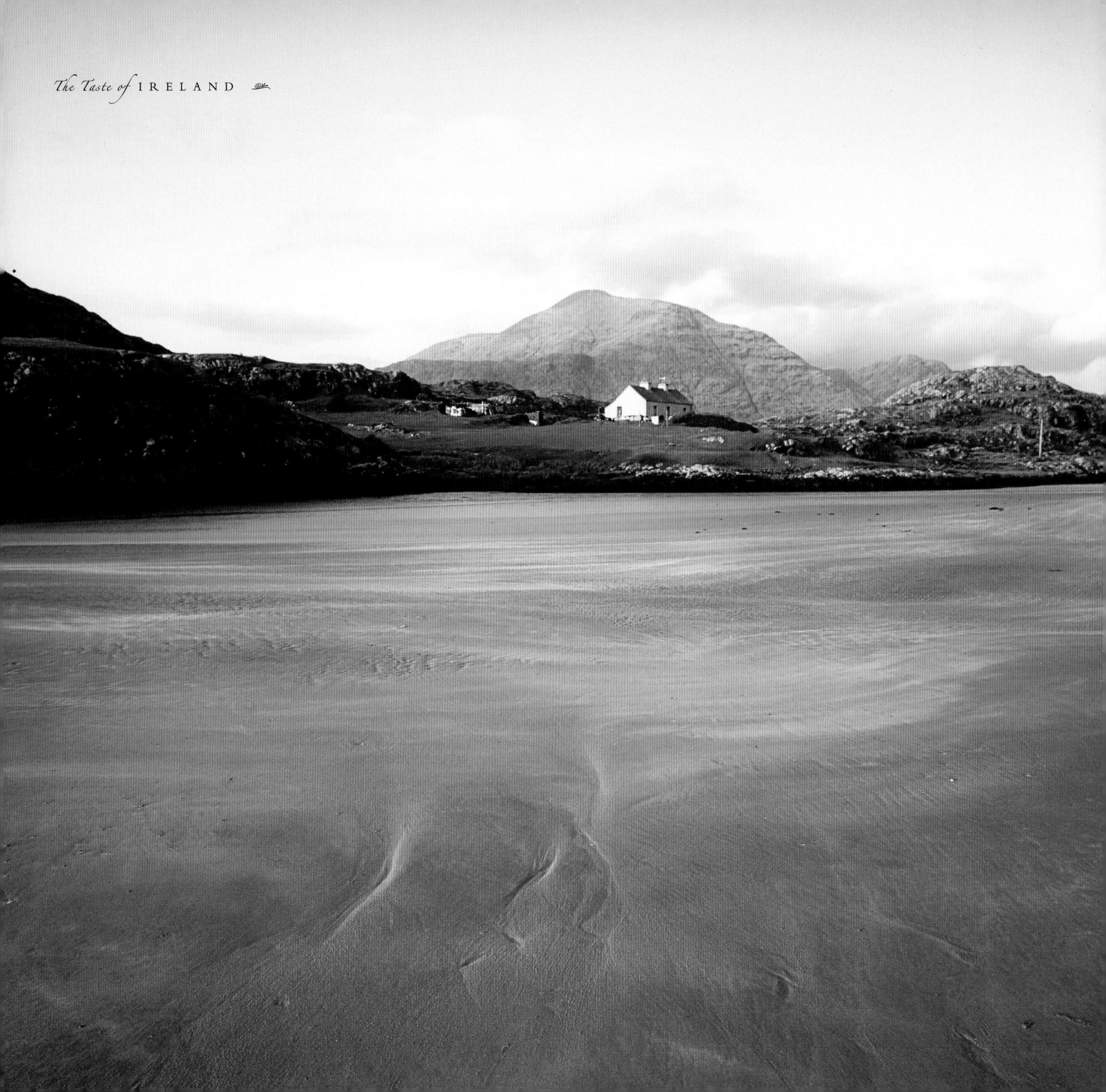

Connemara

Connemara is considered to be one of the last unspoilt areas in Ireland, and much of this county is made up of the Connemara National Park, famous as one of the most beautiful places in the country. The stunning landscape is one of flat, glassy lakes, rugged mountains and lovely coastline and beaches. Poet, playwright and author Oscar Wilde (1854–1900) was certainly moved by its scenery and described Connemara as 'a savage beauty'. The Twelve Bens are a range of jagged quartzite peaks and offer fantastic walking opportunities, with striking views across much of the national park, including the tranquil Lough Inagh. While further north and into Mayo County is the majestic Mweelrea Mountain, which at 814 m (2,670 ft) is the highest peak in Connacht.

Clifden is the largest town in Connemara and it is near here that the entrance to the National Park can be found. Around

Kylemore Abbey, County Galway
Next page: Lough Inagh and the Twelve Bens, County Galway

Clifden there are many megalithic monuments and tombs. Much of this area was also once part of the magnificent Kylemore Abbey and Castle estate. Built from the famous Connemara marble in 1863 for the English politician Mitchell Henry (1826–1910), the castle was turned into a Benedictine monastery in 1920, and later became a secondary girls' boarding school. Other notable sites in the area are the eighteenth-century Ballynahinch Castle, whose history is inextricably bound to Connemara and her people, and Inishboffin Island off the west coast of Galway, which is a breeding ground for many breeds of bird including the rare corncrake.

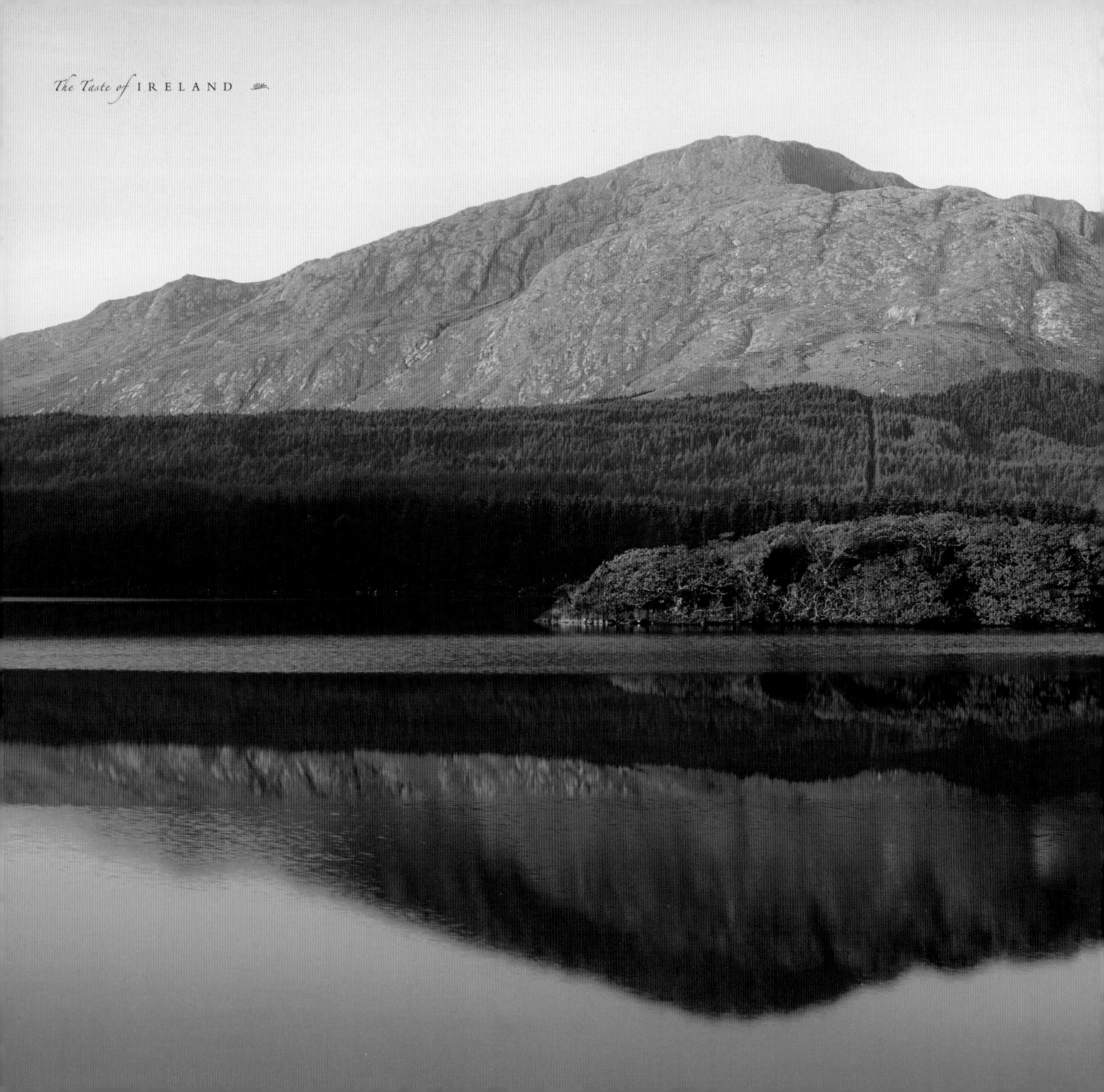

Traditional Galway

The name of Galway is derived from the Irish 'Abhainn na Gaillimhe', meaning River Galway, which in turn was named after the mythological princess Galvia. She is said to have been the daughter of the leader of a Fir Bolg tribe in pre-Celtic times, who drowned in Lough Corrib. As a memorial the river was named after her.

County Galway is divided by Lough Corrib, a huge and beautiful lake that extends in a north/south direction. To the east of Corrib much of the landscape sweeps away into rich and fertile farmland broken up by densely wooded areas that support a timber industry. Here cattle graze on the abundant grasses, hay crops grow in golden swatches and peat is cut for industrial use in power stations, for domestic

Cottages, Tullycross

heating and for garden use. Although farms exist on a large and commercial scale, Galway is also famed for its small-scale domestic farms, many of which employ traditional farming methods. The landscape is also dotted with typical Irish farm cottages, small, often white-washed, sporting colourful front doors and thatched roofs. The simple, but aesthetic quality of these small homes has led to them being used as material for many photographic books charting the rural charms of Galway.

While the cities of Ireland have expanded and become modern cosmopolitan centres, much of the countryside has remained steeped in traditional values. There is a historic, yester-year feel to the landscape of Ireland, and in particular to the relatively isolated and wild area of Galway. It is possibly this sense of quiet, unrefined beauty and life at a slower place that has made much of the Irish countryside so popular with visitors.

County Mayo

Clew Bay and Croagh Patrick

County Mayo can be found to the north-west of County Galway and is the third largest county in Ireland. Despite her size, like Galway she remains largely undeveloped and has a low population. The north and west of Mayo are defined by a rugged mountainous landscape with jagged peaks reflected in the many serene lakes of the area, while fertile farmland can be found towards the east. There is a little bit of something for everyone in Mayo, with scenery ranging from dramatic cliffs to sandy beaches, and from wild, open moorland to the dark bog lands of Ceide Fields in the north. Bog excavations have yielded evidence of a

farming system that dates back some 5,000 years.

County Mayo has strong connections with St Patrick, the patron saint of Ireland, who is said to have fasted for 40 days and nights on the mountain known as Croagh Patrick. During this time, he banished the large colonies of birds that lived there because they contained the demons of paganism and were trying to distract him from his fast. He invited instead angelic birds who soothed him with their songs. The mountain towers above Clew Bay on the western coast of Mayo, which contains excellent examples of sunken drumlins, elongated glacial hills and many tiny islands.

Achill Island

County Sligo

The north of Connacht is largely taken up by County Sligo, known as 'Yeats County'. The poet William Butler Yeats (1865–1939) spent a large portion of his childhood here amongst the spectacular scenery of mountains and beaches, and it was to have a lasting effect on him. He often spoke of his love for the area and its spectacular beauty, and immortalised the Isle of Innisfree in Lough Gill through his poem of the same name. Yeats was also very moved by the loaf-shaped mountain Ben Bulben, which rises steeply from the surrounding landscape outside the village of Drumcliffe. Shortly before the end of his life, Yeats wrote the poem *Under Ben Bulben*, and he is buried not far away in the cemetery at Drumcliffe.

Just a few miles from the town of Sligo and forming a virtual triangle with Ben Bulben is Carrowmore, the second largest megalithic cemetery in Europe. The site has suffered fairly substantial damage, but there remains evidence of over 60 graves, tombs and monuments dating to around 3,000 years ago. To the west of Sligo town is the dominant bulk of Knocknarea. The summit of the mountain is home to a number of megalithic tombs, the most impressive of which at 55 m (180 ft) across and 10 m (33 ft) high is Queen Meabh's. Many stories have been woven around this queen, who has become the fabric of legends, although it is possible she did exist. The number of tombs on this mountain indicates it was an important place in pre-Christian times and would have been a focal point for ritual and ceremonies.

Sculpture of William Butler Yeats, Sligo

Culture

CONNACHT is part of the area known as the Gaeltacht, where Irish is the predominant language. In Connacht the Gaeltacht covers much of Country Galway, including the Aran Islands, and County Mayo. Irish heritage is celebrated here through many festivals and events, such as the internationally famous Galway Arts Festival, a showcase for both traditional and modern Irish music. Of a different nature is the Ballinasloe Horse Fair in County Galway, one of the oldest of its kind in the world.

A more recent festival, but nonetheless just as colourful, is the Galway Oyster Festival, which has taken place every September since 1954. Oysters abound during the festivities, as well as music, dancing and the consumption of large quantities of Guinness. Of a more sporting nature is the traditional *Cruinniú na mBád*, or Gathering of Boats, held at Kinvarra. This festival celebrates the traditional Galway hooker boats that were used to transport peat between Galway and the north of County Clare, and sees the harbour filled with the brightly coloured sail boats.

In the north of Connacht in County Sligo there is a rich literary tradition that traces back to William Butler Yeats, arguably the county's most famous resident. Today the Sligo Arts Festival takes place every summer and celebrates the arts, literature and traditional Irish music. To the west of County Sligo is County Mayo, where traditional Irish culture and music is also strongly recognised, particularly in the town of Mohill. It was here that the famous harpist Turlough O'Carolan (1670–1738) lived for some years, and there is now a statue in the town erected in his honour.

Boats & Sailing

A great deal of Connacht is coastal, while her inland areas are covered with a network of rivers and lakes. Consequently, much of Connacht's thriving tourist industry centres on outdoor pursuits such as water sports, walking, riding, golf and rock climbing, as well as attracting visitors to her rich culture and history.

Roscommon is one of the less publicised of Connacht's counties, but is home to some of the region's best water sports.

The River Shannon and Lough Ree run through the east of the county and the River Suck travels through the west, while to the north is Lough Key, all of which provide outstanding boating and fishing. Equally, Country Leitrim offers endless water-based activities on and around the great Shannon-Erne waterway.

Boating activities often feature in Connacht's festival programme, with the annual boat race at Roundstone in County Galway being an especially lively event. Another event with its roots in tradition is the *Cruinniú na mBád*, or Gathering of Boats, held at Kinvarra, also in County Galway. This sea-port village once boasted a healthy trade in peat between Galway and the north of County Clare, with the peat transported across the waters in traditional Galway hooker boats. These boats, which are inherently beautiful with their simple shape and dark red sails, were designed specifically for the rough waters off the coast of Ireland.

Boat race, Roundstone, County Galway

Traditional Music

Music, traditional and modern, plays a central role in Irish life and culture. The history of music in Ireland is likely to date back to very early times, and probably evolved alongside dance at pagan rituals and ceremonies. It is from these ancient roots that traditional Irish music has emerged in its present form, which today has a huge and dedicated following.

Traditional music is kept alive and celebrated throughout Ireland in both her rural and cosmopolitan areas, primarily through festivals such as the O'Carolan Harp and Traditional Music Festival, which takes place annually at Keadue, County Roscommon, and is named after the famous harpist Turlough O'Carolan who is buried in the town's cemetery. Another is the Louisburgh *Feile Chois Cuain* festival at Louisburgh, County Mayo, which celebrates traditional music, song, dance and *craic*, an Irish term meaning 'enjoyment'. Traditional Irish music also enjoys a great following in the United States of America, and many Irish music festivals take place annually across the States.

The culture of music is also supported through competitions and classes that aim to encourage young people to learn the traditional ways. The *Fleadh Cheoil* (Festival of Music) does just that, and is an Irish music competition held nationwide. County and regional competitions are held to allow entrants to qualify for entry into the prestigious finals. The events aim to establish a level of standards in Irish music as well as celebrating Irish music. Many of the competitions also include parades and festivities, and provide an important meeting place for musicians.

Turlough O'Carolan Statue, Mohill, County Leitrim

Connacht Festivals & Fairs

There are few sights quite so spectacular as the famous Ballinasloe Horse Fair in County Galway, offering a nostalgic and celebratory slice of Irish cultural life. The fair is one of the oldest of its kind in the world, and was for many years also the largest in Europe. Its roots trace far back into history and are largely undocumented until the 1700s. The fair began as a general agricultural event, but from the early twentieth century it evolved to become primarily a horse event. It is held every October and runs for over a week, with the programme including a horse sale and horse shows, parades, dancing, music and general merriment. Many thousands of people turn out for the occasion and hundreds of horses can be seen, in seeming chaos, to mill around the event area.

Galway City, the only city in Connacht, is a thriving centre for culture and arts. The city hosts innumerable festivals and fairs, with the annual Galway Arts Festival in July being one of the country's most popular. The festival runs for two weeks and hosts traditional and modern artistic and cultural events, showcasing theatre acts, traditional and modern music, dance, parades, crafts and lots more.

Another of Galway's immensely popular festivals is the annual Racing Festival, which is held from the last Monday in July for seven days. The race meet offers some of the finest racing in Ireland with something to appeal to every racegoer. It is also a high point on the social calender and is as much about the festivities as it is the horses.

Galway during the Galway Arts Festival

Galway Oyster Festival

Traditional Irish dance at the Galway Oyster Festival

The oyster festival was the brain-child of Brian Collins, the manager of the Great Southern Hotel in Galway City, and came to him as a means to promote his flagging hotel business and attract tourists to the area. During discussions with his chef, the idea of putting oysters on the menu was mooted, and Collins decided to organise a celebration to mark the start of the oyster season. He collaborated with Paddy Burke of Clarinbridge, and they decided to hold the first festival in 1954, at Burke's Clarinbridge pub. The inaugral oyster banquet had just 34 guests, but from these humble beginnings the festival has grown to be one of the largest of its kind in the world, and in 1984 was moved to Galway City, although an oyster festival is still also held in Clarinbridge. In 2000 the Galway International Oyster Fair was voted one of the twelve greatest shows on Earth by the English *The Sunday Times*.

The Galway Oyster Festival is one of the more unusual festivals to occur in the area, and is not dissimilar to the famous Bantry Mussel Fair, in Bantry, Country Cork in the far south of Ireland. It is not the county's only oyster festival, for just to south the of Galway City another oyster fair is held in the small town of Clarinbridge, which is famous for the quality of its oysters. The Clarinbridge event was the original oyster fair in the area, however the Galway Festival is the larger and now the more famous of the two.

Oysters on the Half-shell

SERVES 2–4

INGREDIENTS

24 Galway oysters, in the shell

crushed ice and dulse or dillisk (soaked if dried), to garnish

soda bread and butter, and lemon wedges, to serve

1 Use a blunt-ended oyster knife to shuck the oysters: insert the end of the knife between the shells near the hinge and work it until you cut through the muscle that holds the shells together. Catch the oyster liquid in a bowl.

2 When the oysters are all open, discard the flat shells. Divide the oysters, in the deep halves, among four serving plates lined with crushed ice and soaked dulse.

3 Strain the reserved liquid over the oysters. Serve with the lemon wedges.

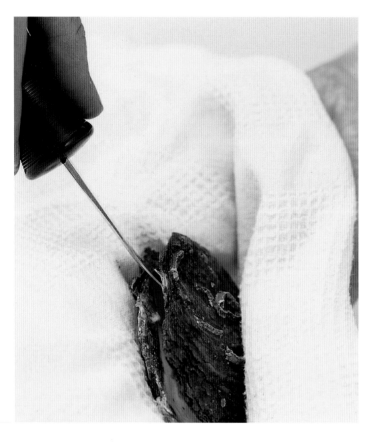

ORIGINS AND TRADITIONS

Oysters are abundant on the west coast of Ireland. The Galway Oyster Festival is the largest of numerous oyster festivals to celebrate this traditional Irish food.

Michelmas Goose

SERVES 6–8

INGREDIENTS

1 goose, 4.5kg/10lb, with giblets

1 onion, sliced

2 carrots, sliced

2 celery sticks, sliced

small bunch of parsley and thyme

450g/1lb black pudding/blood sausage, crumbled or chopped

2 large, tart cooking apples, peeled, cored and finely chopped

1 large garlic clove, crushed

250ml/8fl oz/1 cup dry/hard cider

15ml/1 tbsp plain/all-purpose flour

salt and ground black pepper

1 Remove the liver from the giblets and put the remainder into a pan with the onion, carrots, celery and herbs. Cover with cold water, season and simmer for 30–45 minutes to make a stock for the gravy. Preheat the oven to 200°C/400°F/Gas 6.

2 Meanwhile, chop the liver finely and mix it with the black pudding, garlic and apples. Add salt and ground pepper, and then sprinkle in 75ml/2½fl oz/⅓ cup cider to bind.

3 Wipe out the goose and stuff it with this mixture. Prick the skin with a fork, sprinkle with salt and pepper and rub in.

4 Weigh the stuffed goose and calculate the cooking time at 15 minutes per 450g/1lb and 15 minutes over. Put the goose on a rack in a large roasting pan, cover with foil and put it into the preheated oven.

5 After 1 hour, remove the goose from the oven and carefully pour off the hot fat that has accumulated in the bottom of the pan; reserve this fat for cooking. Pour the remaining dry cider over the goose and return to the oven.

6 Half an hour before the end of the estimated cooking time, remove the foil and carefully baste the goose with the juices.

7 Return to the oven, uncovered, and allow the bird to brown, basting occasionally. When cooked, transfer to a heated serving dish and put it in a warm place to rest.

8 To make the gravy pour off any excess fat from the roasting pan, leaving 30ml/2 tbsp, then sprinkle in enough flour to absorb it. Cook over a medium heat for a minute. Strain the giblet stock and stir in enough to make the gravy. Bring it to the boil and simmer for a few minutes, stirring constantly. Add any juices that have accumulated under the goose, season to taste and pour into a sauceboat. Serve with the carved goose.

Soda Bread

MAKES 1 LOAF

INGREDIENTS

400 g/14 oz/3 cups plain/all purpose flour, plus 1 tbsp
  for dusting
1 tsp salt
2 tsp bicarbonate of/baking soda
1 tbsp butter
50 g/2 oz/⅔ cup coarse oatmeal
1 tsp clear honey
300 ml/½ pint/1¼ cups buttermilk
2 tbsp milk

WHOLEMEAL VARIATION:

400 g/14 oz plain/3 cups wholemeal flour, plus 1 tbsp
  for dusting
1 tbsp milk

1 Preheat the oven to 200°C/400°F/Gas Mark 6, 15 minutes before baking. Sift the flour, salt and bicarbonate of/baking soda into a large bowl. Rub in the butter until the mixture resembles fine breadcrumbs. Stir in the oatmeal and make a well in the centre.

2 Mix the honey, buttermilk and milk together and add to the dry ingredients. Mix to a soft dough.

3 Knead the dough on a lightly floured surface for 2–3 minutes, until the dough is smooth. Shape into a 20.5 cm/8 inch round and place on an oiled baking sheet.

4 Thickly dust the top of the bread with flour. Using a sharp knife, cut a deep cross on top, going about halfway through the loaf.

5 Bake in the preheated oven on the middle shelf of the oven for 30–35 minutes or until the bread is slightly risen, golden and sounds hollow when tapped underneath. Cool on a wire rack. Eat on the day of making.

6 For a wholemeal soda bread, use all the wholemeal flour instead of the white flour and add an extra tablespoon of milk when mixing together. Dust the top with wholemeal flour and bake.

ORIGINS AND TRADITIONS
Soda bread is a staple of the Irish diet and dates back to approximately 1840, when bicarbonate of/baking soda was introduced to Ireland.

Brotchan Foltchep

SERVES 4

INGREDIENTS

50 g/2 oz/½ stick butter

450 g/1 lb/4 cups trimmed, finely sliced leeks

4–5 potatoes, peeled, roughly chopped

900 ml/1½ pints/scant 1 quart vegetable stock

4 fresh rosemary sprigs

450 ml/¾ pint/1¾ cups full-cream/whole milk

2 tbsp freshly chopped parsley

2 tbsp crème fraîche/sour cream

salt and freshly ground black pepper

1 Melt the butter in a large saucepan, add the leeks and cook gently for 5 minutes, stirring frequently. Remove 1 tablespoon of the cooked leeks and reserve for garnishing.

2 Add the potatoes, vegetable stock, rosemary sprigs and milk. Bring to a boil, then reduce the heat, cover and simmer gently for 20–25 minutes, or until the vegetables are tender.

3 Cool for 10 minutes. Discard the rosemary, then pour into a food processor or blender and blend well to form a smooth-textured soup.

4 Return the soup to the cleaned saucepan. Stir in the chopped parsley and crème fraîche/sour cream. Season to taste with salt and pepper. If the soup is too thick, stir in a little more milk or water. Reheat gently without boiling, then ladle into warm soup bowls. Garnish the soup with the reserved leeks. Serve.

ORIGINS AND TRADITIONS

Named after the Irish for 'broth' and 'leeks', this soup has been served in Ireland for generations. Sometimes thickened with oatmeal, many cooks now combine leeks with potatoes, as in this recipe.

Irish Stew

SERVES 4

INGREDIENTS

900g/2 lb neck of lamb cutlets

675g/1½ lb/¾ cups potatoes, peeled and sliced

2 large onions, sliced

salt and freshly ground pepper

1 tbsp parsley and thyme

1 Trim the excess fat off the lamb cutlets. Layer the meat, potatoes and onion with plenty of seasoning and the herbs, in a large or deep ovenproof casserole, finishing with potato.

2 Preheat the oven to 150°C/300°F/Gas Mark 2. Pour on 300–450ml/½ pint–¾ pint water and cover with a tight fitting lid or baking parchment. Cook for about 2 hours, or until the meat and potatoes are tender.

3 Increase the heat to brown off the potatoes at the end of cooking, or cool and heat through the following day at 200°C/400°F/Gas Mark 6, for about 20 minutes. It is best to make it a day in advance, then you can remove any fat that rises to the top and reheat it in a hot oven, browning off the potatoes well at the same time.

ORIGINS AND TRADITIONS

This quintessentially Irish dish is a filling, flavourful peasant meal made with what were the cheapest, most readily available ingredients.

Index

Page numbers in *italics* indicate illustrations.